NEW LESBIAN WRITING

NEW LESBIAN WRITING

An Anthology Edited by
MARGARET CRUIKSHANK

Grey Fox Press
San Francisco

Library of Congress Cataloging in Publication Data

Main entry under title:

New lesbian writing.

    Bibliography: p. 184
    1. Lesbianism—Literary collections. 2. American
literature—Women authors. 3. American literature—20th
century. 4. English literature Women authors.
5. English literature—20th century. I. Cruikshank,
Margaret L.
PS509.L47N48   1984   810'.8'0353   83-22603
ISBN 0-912516-81-X (pbk.)

Distributed by Subterranean Company, P.O. Box 10233,
Eugene, OR 97440.

CONTENTS

PROSE

INTRODUCTION

This is an exciting time for lesbian writing and publishing in the United States. The creation of Kitchen Table: Women of Color Press, the rediscovery of Ann Bannon, the rapid growth of Naiad Press, the publication of Audre Lord's autobiographical work *Zami*, the expansion of women's bookstores, the increasing use of lesbian books in women's studies classes, the readings and panels devoted to lesbian literature at the annual meetings of the National Women's Studies Association, and the papers on lesbian topics read at conventions of the Modern Language Association are all signs of the vitality of lesbian literature in the 1980s.[1]

Today the existence of a large audience for lesbian literature is much more obvious than it was in the mid-seventies, and the subject itself has a legitimacy that would have been hard to foresee ten years ago.[2] As Jane Gapen says in her introductory note to Barbara Deming's story in this anthology, lesbianism "was not considered an authentic hold upon reality" when Barbara was writing in the 1950s. Although the women's movement has vigorously challenged that assumption, it lives on. Today we can laugh at the lurid descriptions of lesbians in older literature, at the ending of "The Fox," for example, in which D. H. Lawrence has a tree fall on a lesbian character, or at a Greek scholar's insistence that Sappho could not have been a lesbian because no pervert could have loved wildflowers as passionately as she did.[3] But many of our contemporaries are still influenced by anti-lesbian bias of a less obvious kind. Consequently, lesbian writing necessarily serves a political and educational purpose regardless of its content, its quality, or the intention of its creators.

Academics have produced much of the lesbian literature published since the early 1970s, and a new generation of lesbian writers, critics, graduate students, and scholars has appeared in the 1980s. On the other hand, grassroots sources have been equally important in the making, preservation, and dissemination of lesbian literature. Examples are the periodicals run by editorial collectives such as *Feminary*, *Conditions*, and *Common*

Lives/*Lesbian Lives* and institutions like the Lesbian Herstory Archives in New York and the West Coast Lesbian Collections in Oakland.[4]

The implications of the new visibility of lesbian literature extend far beyond the gay community itself. The pretentions to universality of traditional literature are more easily exposed now that a significant quantity of lesbian writing is available. In studies of women's literature, critics can now more readily focus on *all* passionate connections between women. More honest literary biographies will be written if lesbian feelings and experiences are acknowledged, and the heterosexist bias of earlier biographies will be clear.[5] Alice Walker's Pulitzer Prize for *The Color Purple* suggests that writers may now be able to explore lesbian themes directly without having their work taken as autobiographical statement. If lesbian themes had appeared in Willa Cather's work, she would not have received a Pulitzer in the 1920s. More recently, in her courageous if rather muted coming out statement *Mrs. Stevens Hears the Mermaids Singing* (1965), May Sarton did not use the word "lesbian"; no context existed then for using the word positively. Today, although the term "tradition" is perhaps too inflated to describe what lesbian feminist writers have created since the sixties, we do have a sizeable body of work to discuss, from the past as well as the present.

A marked trend toward specialization has appeared in the lesbian literature of the 1980s. Instead of assuming the commonality of our experience, as we readily did in the 1970s, we are stressing our differences, in anthologies such as *This Bridge Called My Back: Writings by Radical Women of Color; Nice Jewish Girls: a Lesbian Anthology; Compañeras: Antologia Lesbiana Latina; Home Girls: a Black Feminist Anthology;* and *A Gathering of Spirit*, a special issue of *Sinister Wisdom* on North American Indian Women.[6] Work in progress carries forward this investigation of our origins, particular subgroups, or special interests; for example, writings by working-class women, a collection of autobiographical stories and essays by lesbian nuns and former nuns, and an anthology on lesbian history.[7]

Definitions of lesbian literature have proved elusive. Do we mean writing about lesbian identity or experience by women who call themselves lesbians? If a lesbian writes a story or poem about another subject, is it lesbian literature? Do we include work by heterosexual writers with lesbian themes and characters? New Lesbian Writing includes examples of the first two categories, and the story by Ethel Florence Lindsay Richardson, an Australian writer who used the pseudonym Henry Handel Richardson, should perhaps be assigned to the third. Such distinctions, meaningless for most of the twentieth century because almost all lesbian writers have been closeted, become important when classes in gay literature or lesbian literature are being developed.

This anthology was originally conceived as a text for lesbian and gay literature classes that would include several genres. As I began to gather material I saw a broader potential audience — students taking classes in women's studies, ethnic studies, or contemporary culture, and lesbians and gay men in general. Since very little autobiography or fiction by older women has been published, and since older lesbians are only now becoming visible, the selections by four lesbian writers over sixty-five may interest readers otherwise not likely to pick up a volume of gay or lesbian literature. By providing a rather full bibliography and these introductory notes, I hope nevertheless to make New Lesbian Writing especially useful to students and teachers.

The word "new" in the title has several meanings: writing by women who have not appeared in print before or who are not yet well known, unpublished work by established writers, and work from other countries new to American readers. "Two Hanged Women," for example, the story by Henry Handel Richardson, was published earlier in England and Australia but has never before been published in the United States. The forms chosen by contributors to this anthology, though not new, suggest some possibilities for future lesbian writing: the fable, the short sketch of a single character or incident, the meditative prose poem, the journal entry, the autobiographical tale framed by classical myths, the personal narrative that incorporates social criticism and philosophical asides, and the story of a writer's development.

In looking through the poetry submitted to this anthology, Ida Red, the poetry editor, and I found a variety of styles, wry humor and playfulness, and more family themes than we would have expected. Predictably many poems are love poems. Others make political statements. Several poets reflect on identity and transitions in their lives. If a search for roots seems to characterize both the poetry and the prose sections of *New Lesbian Writing*, the reason may be that our need to heal ourselves, partly through writing, is more obvious now than in the 1970s, when many of us felt like missionaries carrying the good news of lesbian feminism wherever we went. The euphoria of those days has given way to more somber assessments of our situation. Clearly the identity of lesbian feminist, empowering as it is, has not fulfilled all of our emotional and spiritual needs. Thus the quest theme will probably remain a significant one in our work.

If at times in the 1980s the ideal of sisterhood has seemed tarnished, as we recognize that we have sometimes turned our harshest anger on each other, trounced women writers mercilessly in book reviews, and sapped our energy by feuding, we have kept *visions* of women bonding, even when we have found the mere celebration of lesbianism no longer fruitful. Thus disillusionment, though present in *New Lesbian Writing*, is not a predominant theme.

With its roots in the women's movement, lesbian literature has developed independently of gay male literature. Readers familiar with recently published work by and about men, *Cracks in the Image*, for example, *On the Line*, or *Couplings*, will find this anthology very different in spirit.[8] The most obvious contrast is the pervasiveness of explicitly sexual themes in gay male writing. Students often comment, too, that lesbian literature is more political and less likely to have an urban setting. The coming out experience is more emphasized in lesbian writing than in writing by men. Common to both, however, is a sense of irony, an often comic apprehension of the gulf separating who we are from who we were supposed to be.

A gulf of another kind, between the ideas of good writing held by some traditionally-educated lesbian writers and critics and the quality of much of the work produced so far, should be acknowledged. Those who raise questions of standards and excellence, however, sail into dangerous waters where accusations of patriarchal elitism await them. Since the identity of writer empowers women, it is difficult to challenge anyone's claim to that identity or to set aside the feminist principle that our work should be understandable to all. Writers belonging to any group with a political agenda, of course, face the sometimes conflicting demands of art and politics and the question of self-censorship. For lesbians, these issues are fairly recent compared to the old problem of invisibility.

If the work collected here suggests a new complexity in lesbian literature, we may be coming to the end of a period in which we were necessarily parochial in our concerns, because survival demanded that we focus on the meaning of our emotional and sexual identities. But even though we can now turn more easily to other subjects, as Audre Lorde does in *Zami*, for example, and Mary Meigs in *Lily Briscoe: a Self-Portrait*, the struggle to become whole women still continues to preoccupy us.

In *My Thirty Years War*, the first of her three autobiographies, Margaret Anderson tells how she, her lover Jane Heap, and a few friends decided to pitch tents on the shore of Lake Michigan when their rent money ran out. They camped for several months, washing their clothes in the lake and traveling miles each day to their jobs in the Loop. Less boldly and publicly eccentric than Margaret and Jane, lesbian writers today are nonetheless intrepid, as we must be to speak in our own voices in a homophobic culture. The rich diversity of those voices can only be suggested by *New Lesbian Writing*.

NOTES

1. The address of Kitchen Table is Box 592, Van Brunt Station, Brooklyn, New York, 11215. Ann Bannon's lesbian pulp novels of the 1950s have recently been reprinted by Naiad Press. See the bibliography for titles. Naiad's address is Box 10543, Tallahassee, FL 32302.
2. Alfred A. Knopf, the publisher of Jill Johnston's autobiographical *Mother Bound* in 1983, probably would not have published her *Lesbian Nation* in 1975.
3. David M. Robinson, *Sappho and Her Influence* (Boston: Marshall Jones Company, 1924), p. 44.
4. Other important lesbian periodicals are *Focus*, edited by Paula Bennett, and *Sinister Wisdom*, edited by Michelle Cliff and Adrienne Rich. At the Collections and the Archives, women can find out-of-print books and periodicals; examine unpublished manuscripts; leave copies of their own work; browse through books from other countries; hear oral histories; and attend presentations by artists, writers, and historians.
5. Jean Strouse's biography of Alice James, for example (Houghton Mifflin, 1980), is excellent except for its failure to investigate the partnership of Alice James and Katharine Loring. It is the biographer's unwillingness to do this, as much as her ignoring of lesbian evidence, that reveals her heterosexist bias. See also Blanche Cook's review essay on *The Life of Lorena Hickock, E.R.'s Friend*, by Doris Faber, in *Feminist Studies* 6 (Fall 1980), 511-516.
6. Both *This Bridge Called My Back* (1981), edited by Cherríe Moraga and Gloria Anzaldúa, and *Nice Jewish Girls* (1982), edited by Evelyn Beck, were published by Persephone Press. *Compañeras* is being compiled by the Colectiva Lesbiana Latinoamericana in New York. *Home Girls*, edited by Barbara Smith, was published in 1983 by Kitchen Table. Other works include *Cuentos: Stories by Latinas*, edited by Alma Gomez, Cherríe Moraga, and Mariana Romo-Carmona (Kitchen Table, 1983); Becky Birtha's collection of stories, *For Nights Like*

This One (Frog in the Well, 1983); Anita Cornwell's Black Lesbian in White America, political essays and autobiographical writing; and Paula Gunn Allen's novel The Woman Who Owned the Shadows (Spinster's, Ink, 1983). A chapter from the novel appears in this anthology.

7. Pam Annas is editing an anthology of writing by working-class women. The convent lesbian stories, tentatively titled Breaking Silence, edited by Nancy Manahan and Rosemary Curb, will be published by Naiad. Frances Doughty is the editor of the history collection Lesbian Tapestry. Another important future publication is A Barbara Deming Reader: the Development of her Thinking on Feminism and Nonviolent Struggle, by New Society Publishers.

8. Cracks in the Image: Stories by Gay Men (Gay Men's Press, 1981); On the Line: New Gay Fiction, edited by Ian Young (The Crossing Press, 1981); The Gay Touch, short stories by Peter Robins (Crossing, 1982); and Couplings: a Book of Stories by Richard Hall (Grey Fox Press, 1981).

Note: for background on lesbian literature see Jane Rule, Lesbian Images (The Crossing Press, 1983; originally published in 1975); Lillian Faderman, Surpassing the Love of Men: Romantic Friendship and Love Between Women from the Renaissance to the Present (William Morrow, 1981); Barbara Grier, The Lesbian in Literature, 3rd ed. (Naiad Press, 1981); Elly Bulkin's introduction to the anthologies Lesbian Fiction and Lesbian Poetry (Persephone, 1981); Bertha Harris, "What We Mean to Say: Notes Towards Defining the Nature of Lesbian Literature" (Heresies 3, Fall 1977); and Bonnie Zimmerman, "Is 'Chloe Liked Olivia' a Lesbian Plot?" (Women's Studies International Forum 6 [1983]: 169-175). Several essays on literature appear in my anthology Lesbian Studies (The Feminist Press, 1982).

ACKNOWLEDGMENTS

I thank the following publishers for reprint permission: Alfred A. Knopf for Marilyn Hacker's poem "How It Happens," from *Taking Notice* (New York, 1980); Angus & Robertson for Henry Handel Richardson's story "Two Hanged Women," from *The Adventures of Cuffy Mahony* (Sydney, 1979); *Fireweed* for Jane Rule's article "Making the Real Visible: Lesbian and Writer" (Issue #13), 1982); The Gay Presses of New York for the translation by Karla Jay and Yvonne Klein of Renée Vivien's story "Prince Charming," from *Women of the Wolf* (1983); *IKON* for Beth Brant's story "A Simple Act" (Summer/Fall 1983); Iridian Press for the title story of LindaJean Brown's *jazz dancin wif mama* (New York, 1981); and Sheba Feminist Publishers for Suniti Namjoshi's fables "The Example," "Troglodyte," "The Mouse and the Lion," and "The Badge-Wearing Dyke and her Two Maiden Aunts," from *Feminist Fables* (London, 1981).

The selection by Mary Meigs is taken from her forthcoming *The Medusa Head*, which will be published by Talonbooks in Vancouver. A different version of Elsa Gidlow's "Casting a Net" was published in *Feminist Studies* 6 (Spring 1980). The work first appeared in its present form in *The Body Politic*, No. 83 (May 1982) and is reprinted here with permission.

I thank Kay Iseman of the South Australian College of the Arts and Education for calling my attention to Henry Handel Richardson's "Two Hanged Women." Iseman discusses Richardson's work in her dissertation, "The Place of Woman in the Australian Tradition," University of Pittsburgh, 1983.

I thank the Center for Research on Women at Stanford, where I have been an affiliate scholar since 1981, for recognizing the importance of lesbian studies and for giving me an opportunity to revive my Victorian interests and discover new worlds of feminist research.

My contributors deserve special thanks for their patience, cooperation and enthusiasm for this anthology. I feel honored to be entrusted with their work.

I acknowledge the important contributions to lesbian literature of two women not directly connected to this book—Clare Potter of the West Coast Lesbian Collections and Barbara Grier of Naiad Press—who have generously shared with me their literary knowledge.

I am indebted to two colleagues in the English department of the City College of San Francisco, Dan Allen and Jack Collins. Dan first proposed that I teach gay and lesbian literature, co-taught a class with me, and gave me the idea for this anthology. Jack's teaching and wide knowledge of gay literature have been valuable influences on me.

I thank the publisher of Grey Fox, Don Allen, for help of various kinds and for showing me, by skillful example, how a good publisher works.

Ida VSW Red brought her considerable editing skills and knowledge of feminist process to the task of selecting poetry for this anthology. I thank her for her significant contribution to *New Lesbian Writing*.

My typist, Judy Freespirit, a writer herself, was a pleasure to work with.

Finally, I thank two particular friends, Matile Poor and Nancy Manahan, who are spiritually part of any work I undertake. For help with some of the editing of *New Lesbian Writing*, I am especially grateful to Nancy.

—Margaret Cruikshank

NEW LESBIAN WRITING

MARTHA COURTOT

Each Morning

each morning
i return to the sea
taking from the sand
the refuse of the night

today for instance
everything i find is black—
black coral
a black shell
fine as the face of an old lover
black stones
and little pieces of glass
black as night

yesterday i found
shapes of fishes
in everything i touched
and things that had left their feet behind
as if they had learned a new way to get around
which i took as a personal message
but could not quite decipher

tomorrow is still dark on the horizon
ceaseless the sea returns to us
all lost things

if i am drifting today
somewhere far out
beyond any hope of finding
my throat drying up

my hands turning into water, into waves
still i know i will be found
tomorrow   on some shore

perhaps by a fisherwoman
out early for the sun on her breasts
or by a triad of doves
mourning the loss of night
at the sea's edge

and i will come
bearing my own gifts from the sea
and wearing on my face
the shapes of where i've been
and hidden in the corners of my weary eyes
the tracks of where i'm going

The Lesbian Bears

Here they have not heard of lesbian bears
if they knew they would be afraid
they would form a vigilante party
to hunt wild perverse bears in the mountains

at night while they slept in the open
they would dream of unnatural acts
in brown fur
sleeping in the open a female bear would come
wrapping her arms around the bodies
of all the women
then they too would be lost
is this where lesbians come from?

I have seen lesbian plums which cling to each other
in the tightest of monogamous love
and I have watched lesbian pumpkins
declare the whole patch their playground
profligate & dusky
their voices arouse something in us
which is laughing

ah, everything is lesbian which loves itself
I am lesbian when I really look in the mirror
the world is lesbian in the morning & the evening
only in mid-afternoon does it try to pretend otherwise

and when the lesbian wind flutters the leaves
of the bright lesbian trees
sending golden shudders of delight
through the changing lesbian light
the sound which is returned to you
is only an echo of your own lesbian nature

admit it   you too would like to love yourself
and each other   now, while the vigilantes
wander in the mountains
now is the perfect time

embrace the nearest to you   woman or child
apricot, salmon, artichoke, cow

embrace yourself

Childhood Secret: One

mother, it is night again
all darkness falls upon me

while you sleep, the train steals away my heart
its engine is more powerful than the death of my father
it rides through the dark and intricate centers
of unknowable cities
its eats into the future with its wide loud mouth

oh that song the train sings!
i have opened my veins to its music
forever now i will be a sister to anything that wants
to move away

mother, while i lie here above you
in this my father's bed
my heart has already left with the two a.m. train

in the morning   do not look for me
i have gone to live out my father's life
among strangers

MARILYN HACKER

Alba: January, After Surgery

Tonight when I cup my hand beneath your breast
(fountain and pillow of felicity)
your womb shudders with possibility
suctioned from you, and your sigh is pain. Pressed
even gently against me, you ache; the best
choice, made, presses us both. How will it be
held between us, this complicity
in what we can't repeat? Silken, we nest
aloft, sleep curled. Reflected from the snow,
a dawn lamp glints up through your tall window.
Uptown, my child will wake, ask where's her mother.
Promised, I inhale you, descend from you, gather
scattered woolens, gather my wits to go
from one hard choice, love chosen, to the other.

How It Happens

Really, it's a co-educational
boarding-school. The big girls complain about
the boys: spotty, spoken-for. They do without
those gymnastic recreational
pastimes, compensate in the dining-hall
with Scrabble and lime fizz. One gawky sweet
long-limbed math whiz and one dour Semit-
ic Latin grind are keeping their council
on the topic, trudge in the woods in the rain
instead, get giddy at intramural

events, slope off, slanting, before the bell.
Doors wedged shut in a pink-wallpapered room
they prime their adolescent epicene
genius on specialized curriculum.

Graffiti from the Gare Saint-Manqué

for Zed Bee

Outside the vineyard is a caravan
of Germans taking pictures in the rain.
The local cheese is Brillat-Savarin.
The best white wine is Savigny-les-Beaune.
We learn Burgundies while we have the chance
and lie down under cabbage-rose wallpaper.
It's too much wine and brandy, but I'll taper
off later. Who is watering my plants?
I may go home as wide as Gertrude Stein
—another Jewish Lesbian in France.

Around the sculptured Dukes of Burgundy,
androgynous monastics, faces cowled,
thrust bellies out in marble ecstasy
like child swimmers having their pigtails towelled.
Kids sang last night. A frieze of celebrants
circles the tomb, though students are in school,
while May rain drizzles on the beautiful
headlines confirming François Mitterrand's
election. We have Reagan. Why not be
another Jewish Lesbian in France?

Aspiring Heads of State are literate
here, have favorite poets, can explain
the way structuralists obliterate
a text. They read at night. They're still all men.
Now poppy-studded meadows of Provence
blazon beyond our red sardine-can car.
We hope chairpersons never ask: why are
unblushing deviants abroad on grants?
My project budget listed: Entertain
another Jewish Lesbian in France.

I meant my pithy British village neighbor
who misses old days when sorority
members could always know each other: they wore
short-back-and-sides and a collar and tie.
She did, too. Slavic eyes, all romance
beneath an Eton crop with brilliantined
finger-waves, photographed at seventeen
in a dark blazer and a four-in-hand:
a glimpse of salad days that made the day for
another Jewish Lesbian in France.

Then we went on to peanuts and Campari,
she and her friend, my friend and I, and then
somehow it was nine-thirty and a hurry
to car and *carte* and a carafe of wine,
Lapin Sauté or Truite Meunière in Vence.
Convivial quartet of friends and lovers:
had anyone here dreaded any other's
tears, dawn recriminations and demands?
Emphatically not. That must have been
another Jewish Lesbian in France.

It's hard to be almost invisible.
You think you must be almost perfect too.
When your community's not sizeable,
it's often a community of two,
and a dissent between communicants
is a commuter pass to the abyss.
Authorities who claim you don't exist
would sometimes find you easy to convince.
(It helps if you can talk about it to
another Jewish Lesbian in France.)

A decorated she-Academician
opines we were thought up by horny males.
No woman of equivalent position
has yet taken the wind out of her sails.
(How would her "lifelong companion" have thanked her?)
Man loving Man's *her* subject, without mention
if what they do is due to her invention
—and if I'd been her mother, I'd have spanked her.
(Perhaps in a suppressed draft *Hadrian's*
another Jewish Lesbian in France.)

Then the advocates of Feminitude
—with dashes as their only punctuation—
explain that Reason is to be eschewed:
In the Female Subconscious lies salvation.
Suspiciously like Girlish Ignorance,
it seems a rather watery solution.
If I can't dance, it's not my revolution.
If I can't think about it, I won't dance.
So let the ranks of *Psych et Po* include
another Jewish Lesbian in France.

I wish I had been packed off to the nuns
to learn good manners, Attic Greek, and Latin.
(No public Bronx Junior High School fit all that in.)
My angsts could have been casuistic ones.
It's not my feminist inheritance
to eat roots, drink leaf broth, live in a cave,
and not even know how to misbehave
with just one vowel and five consonants.
This patchwork autodidact Anglophone's
another Jewish Lesbian in France,

following Natalie Barney, Alice B.
Toklas, Djuna Barnes, generous Bryher,
Romaine Brooks, Sylvia Beach, H.D.,
Tamara de Lempicka, Janet Flanner.
They made the best use of the circumstance
that blood and stockings often both were bluish;
(they all were white, and only Alice Jewish)
wicked sept/oct/nonagenarians.
Would it have saved Simone Weil's life to be
another Jewish Lesbian in France?

It isn't sex I mean. Sex doesn't save
anyone, except, sometimes, from boredom
(and the underpaid under-class of whoredom
is often bored at work). I have a grave
suspicion ridicule of Continence
or Chastity is one way to disparage
a woman's choice of any job but marriage.
Most of us understand what we renounce.
(This was a lunchtime peptalk I once gave
another Jewish Lesbian in France

depressed by temporary solitude
but thinking coupled bliss was dubious.)
I mean: one way to love a body viewed
as soiled and soiling existential dross
is knowing through your own experience
a like body embodying a soul
to be admirable and loveable.
That is a source that merits nourishment.
Last night despair dressed as self-loathing wooed
another Jewish Lesbian in France.

The sheet was too soft. Unwashed for three weeks,
it smelled like both of us. The sin we are
beset by is despair. I rubbed my cheeks
against the cotton, thought, I wouldn't care
if it were just *my* funk. Despair expands
to fill . . . I willed my arm: extend; hand: stroke
that sullen shoulder. In the time it took
synapse to realize abstract commands,
the shoulder's owner fell asleep. Still there
another Jewish Lesbian in France

stared at the sickle moon above the skylight,
brooding, equally sullen, that alone
is better after all. As close as my right
foot, even my bed stops being my own.
Could I go downstairs quietly, make plans
for myself, not wake her? Who didn't undress,
slept on the couch bundled with loneliness
rather than brave that nuptial expanse
five weeks before. Another contradiction
another Jewish Lesbian in France

may reconcile more gracefully than I.
We're ill-equipped to be obliging wives.
The post office and travel agency
are significant others in our lives.
Last summer I left flowers at Saint Anne's
shrine. She had daughters. One who, legends tell,
adrift, woman-companioned, shored (is still
revered) in the Camargue, her holy band's
navigatrix, Mary, calming the sea
—another Jewish Lesbian in France?

It says they lived together forty years,
Mary and Mary and Sarah (who was Black).
Unsaintly ordinary female queers,
we packed up and went separately back.
We'd shared the road with Gypsy sleeper vans
to join Sarah's procession to the shore.
Our own month-end anabasis was more
ambiguous. Among Americans
my polyglot persona disappears,
another Jewish Lesbian in France.

Coeur mis à nu in sunlight, khaki pants
I've rolled up in a beach towel so ants
and crickets from the leafage won't invade
their sweaty legs: in a loaned hermit-glade
pine-redolent of New Hampshire, not France,
I disentangle from the snares I laid.
Liver-lobed mushrooms thicken in the shade,
shrubs unwrap, pinelings thrust through mulch. Noon slants
across my book, my chest, its lemonade
rays sticky as a seven-year-old's hands.

New Hampshire/New York
August 1981-February 1982

KAREN BRODINE

They Outlawed Touch

they outlawed touch between those of the same body
no twins, no sisters, no friends or neighbors

   an oddity, the way I wash my hair, the
               way I bare my teeth?

get used to that word perverse
you might as well get used
            to spit in your face

and know pacific as an ocean
just some innocent ocean
          get used to flaunting
          your fists

reach across wall, ice, lock, myth
    across lies we don't exist.

while a candidate swears on a bible he's no queer.

I never knew what I was till I knew my name.   Dyke.

Lesbiana, the young girls jeer,
and I know there must be one among them
swinging her skirt brashly, hearing

her own name, seeing herself
in me
and I have loud   names for this
burnt kiss, singe

secret
risk, pride
stronger tendon
tender
grin
fist   hand   human natural animal hand.

What It Was Like

This is what it was like last time visiting in the living room
facing the tv, first time I've seen dad in months and we watch
the news, and Quincy, cracking some medical mystery.

We sit and stare because it fills the room with words
The news is two lesbians winning their kids in court
and I wonder what he's thinking.

He's a do this do that one, and little rest between,
a dogged, leaning-forward look to him, collecting and discarding
as he goes, a garden, greener than I can imagine,
a daughter, more serious and goofy than he could believe,
a house, a wife, there then gone, exed out,
a barrow, a hoe, a harp and a sketch of joyous mother and child
by Kollwitz.

In that short exhausting visit each year, we are two adults,
queasy with talk, we sit or drive or walk, he cooks overflowing
meals and I hope I can eat enough.

We jounce in his skittery chev toward the beach
under the northerly rush of clouds
and the farther up the shore into silence we walk

the more I see, the more each object
leaps up toward my questions

He combs for driftwood and stone, eyes peeled,
I follow like a sharp-edged shadow,
trying to puzzle the clip of wave, the sand of his hair,
his wind-burnt face, the cliff's steep drop.
Following his feet that bulge and runover in old shoes,
I know suddenly why the images clamour; how all my
   growing life
I have seized on salty stone   coherent shells
gnarled white   wood lying porous in the sun

I have been trying to get the sense of it
squinting to detect what each clue knows
what this one sandal or fraying rope holds
fierce to gather silence thick with feeling
into something I can give.

Irons in the Fire

song for Merle

Both oars in the water
No feet on the ground
You and me in the hammock
Dancing all around

Honey tell me yr stories
Honey tell me yr worries
I've got a bee in my bonnet for you
I've got a singular sonnet for you

One time you woke me at midnight
One time you rocked me at noon
When I think of yr knees and so on
A shiver runs right up my spine

Two hawks up in the fir tree
Four arms wrapped all about
Two heads together
Singing some new joy out

M. S. ANDREWS

How My Love for Her Is Like a Fugue*

A footprint in the sand
candlelight in silver earrings.

I cannot keep the days from passing
white sails unfurling on the bay
a footprint in the sand
dancers twirling across a stage
ice cubes dissolving in a glass
candlelight in silver earrings.

Open the door quickly
the Page of Cups bowing
bringing hope
a footprint in the sand
hidden in a golden goblet
a frog prince
for the Queen of Coins
candlelight in silver earrings.

The Page of Cups bowing
I cannot keep my heart
in the passing
hope hidden in the sand
ice cubes dissolving across a stage
white sails unfurling in a golden goblet
dancers twirling on the bay
a footprint in silver earrings
candlelight in a glass.

And she is like
and she is like
a sail unfurling and
a dancer twirling and
my heart dissolving and
I cannot keep the days from passing
hidden in a golden goblet
a dancer twirling
the Page of Cups
opens the door
the Queen of Coins
I cannot keep
what she is
candlelight in silver earrings.

A footprint
footprint
in the sand
and candlelight
candlelight
in silver earrings.

---

*fugue: a musical composition in which one or two themes are repeated
or imitated by successively entering voices and developed in a con-
tinuous interweaving of the voice parts.

Coming Into My Own

I am having an affair with a woman
who is an old acquaintance.
We've been flirting for a long time
across crowded drunk smoke-filled evenings
at the only women's bar in this town.
Even in my thoughts
she's never been far away.
We discovered each other
recently in a pawnshop
both waiting to be redeemed from the past
and struck a bargain.
Considering the state of my mind
I think I got the better deal.
Her name
is Solitude.

In the late afternoon
she arrives without announcing herself
her long purple cape trailing behind
the petals of dead flowers
falling from her fingers.
From my typewriter she removes
the blank piece of paper
I've been staring at for weeks
and covers the machine with her own clothes.
She is cold
disdainful
and never talks much
a perversely attractive woman.
We collapse in slow motion onto the bed;
she lies between my legs
sinks into me.
Words that are

indistinguishable mumblings
float down upon us from the ceiling
like tickertape.
My lips part for them
as if for a kiss
from a lover much-desired.
The mouth of Solitude covers mine
and it is deep darkness we enter together
oh deep.
Her tongue searches the bruised edges
of my heart
and it closes up
a painful reflex triggered.
Afterward she sleeps and I find
sounds trapped in my throat.

The words will not take no
for an answer.
I make love to myself and
the pen quivers in my hand.
I lay the words on the paper
breathlessly.
There is an urgency in me
to discover how they fit together.
Yet the stroke
of the pen across the paper
is slow and steady.
I know the words left in my mouth
by Solitude
will take their own time
making sense of it.
I fall asleep in her arms
and she is gone by morning
slipping away into the darkness
into her own shadows.

The words are in the air.
Strangers on street corners
hand them to me like pamphlets
prophesying the second coming of Christ.
I am only a scribe
frantically recording what I hear
arranging the sounds
into recognizable patterns.
All my senses have gone
to my head.
I do not hunger for food
or for the human touch.

The words wake me
from a restless sleep.
I am tossed out of a dream
rolling across my double bed
and sitting bolt upright
my mouth full of words
round like marbles.
I wake giving birth
to these words
each one cradled to the page.
The gestation time is over
and I am coming
coming
coming
into my own
life.

ESTHER HAWK

After the School Fire Come Dreams

I screech over lost shoes,
order my son into the car,
run back to the house for the key.
Driving, we do not speak
except about dreams. He says
he doesn't remember any.

In the evening he wheedles time
like candy: Mom, please, I just
want to hear this music, just
want to see what's next. Finally,

he sleeps, and then
his dream, a fire, again. This time
I'm the one who was burning
and he tells me he dreamed it
over and over and couldn't stop.

Visitation Rights

1.

After fifteen months you fly in,
a day late, without a word,
and are surprised by his tears.

You have always been late,
beginning that night when I
labored until morning
and you went home to sleep.
Before dawn I called you, come,
now it is happening, and then
for two hours as the pains
scraped my back I waited, saw you,
car spun sideways on the freeway
and a crowd gathering. "Just in time,"
you laughed, scrambling
into a white gown, but you weren't.

And I hate you for teaching him
to expect so little, so young.

2.

Sometimes he does not
recognize you until you speak.

As I drive him home
in the winter dark he tells me
stories about Orion and his two dogs,
the big one, who is the Daddy,
and the little one forever falling
toward the Daddy's waiting back.

Sometimes he calls me Daddy.

Elm

In every wind storm you dance old-lady dances,
creak and crack, stiff stretches like an aging
Martha Graham trying to dance Clytemnestra:

She trips on her robes,
grasps sideways with her spider hand
but cannot hold the pose.
And we applaud, and cry, as she falls.

Old one, remnant of virgin forest,
sometimes when it rains, at night,
I sing to you a calypso lullaby: lay down,
lay down, lay down and take your rest.
But you are not ready. You stand by my house
sighing, muttering like a bag lady to passersby:
look as I bend, I sag, I break. Look. I am beautiful.

IDA VSW RED

delicate protections

here in the land of no seasons
all seasons conspiring to confuse
we wear both rawhide and silk
next to the skin for protection

redwood suckers rub branches
with golden rain trees
rolling hills are interrupted
only by a superimposed image
of fences strung with barbed wire
a small rectangular reflection
from another perspective
not the dominant vision

here the road, earthier than
O'Keefe's, like hers ends in mystery
not floating over the landscape
rather sunk deeply into ground
surface of hills mere hummocks
to lift off, rearrange like little
mounds of moss in a terrarium

how easily such transpositions
might take place in a life
how many choices there are
for the perceptive eye once
it rests from classifying
comparing, considering time
of year, once it allows itself
to caress the scene, move over

around, away, back again to
seeing, feeling the loved one

here limestone monoliths were
at once smoothed, rounded by
glacial movement and cracked
cratered, pocked, left with
great nipples erect, laced
in lichen, yellow, rust, green,
grey, network of delicate
protections

Tomales Bay, 1981

touch dancing

far from you in the familiar beauty
of this loved valley unknown to you
i smell your skin in newly washed green
your juices in magnolia and wild rose
hear the river sigh my name
in your muted undertone
low variations of the fugue
caressing rounded stone, roughly
smoothed like the heel of your hand
feel your breath in comforting air
softened by altitude and humidity
feared only in brief drafts of pain
between hills in evening and in wisps of
morning fog exposing pockets of doubt
soft air enclosing and nudging me
into light subdued as your gaze, into
gently loving rain on big-leafed

trees, layering sensation on sensation
until I am touch dancing with you
no sense of mystery or distance

JUDY SCHAVRIEN

How the Memories Open Out

if I could thread through the eyes
of my many memories
to emerge again
on your dark blue couch
near your blue-bloused body
in the empty green
of a night in the suburbs
where you no longer live
and no longer breathe
to Ray Charles remembering
Georgia Georgia

if I could find the right thread
through the eye of my memory
ride on the sleekest
silkiest hue of it
back again
raw from the black wind
red from the long drive
warming at long last
to your gold body

if I could climb through that eye
to emerge where the green
unpleating spaces
are falling away
and the full-voiced choir
of Schönberg's dream
in Jacob's Ladder
throbs

as we kiss still listening
throbbing again
its pyramid
toward heaven

then I would twist through that aching
black gap in memory
plunge through an anti-universe
of memory
to emerge again
in the night by the lakeside
simply embracing you
simply embraced
right now this instant
oh darling
oh my darling I would

Intolerance

I married a woman
tall as a three-story house
on the pleasantly curving
canals of Amsterdam

and she's just about perfect
a fine place to live in

except for the times
when she gives me a terrible fright
as her sturdy neck
shoots suddenly up and up
through the night's red rashes
her gold hair flares

like a radar transmitter
and her strong grin splashes
hello
down the dust
of the milky way

except for the times
when I take even greater fright
as her outstretched arms
recoil into stumps of wings
her jawbone puckers
her billowing heart
buckles in & she chars
to a crisp black beetle
that bolts for the doorcrack
out of my myth

it makes me so angry

before I can stop myself
I have raised my foot

PAMELA GRAY

after repeated attempts

after repeated attempts
to get over you

i've decided to just
give up

accept the fact that
fifty years from now

i'll be sitting in a wheelchair
in the Home for Aged Dykes
muttering your name

some cute volunteer
in a dungaree jacket
will pat me on my wrinkled arm
saying, "there, there,
maybe she'll come tomorrow"

my weak heart will flutter
each time a phone rings
or a visitor's announced

oh and i'll get visitors:
all the women i wouldn't
sleep with over the years
because i was waiting
for you

they'll show me pictures
of their collective land
in the country,
their alternatively
reproduced grandchildren

occasionally they may ask,
"have you heard from . . ."
and i'll lower my gray head
"well," they'll say,
"she must be very busy"

at night, rereading
my tattered antique copies
of *Twenty-One Love Poems*
and *Beginning with O*,
looking through the yellowed
photographs of our vacation
in P-town, fifty years back,

i'll ask myself
what it was about you

and i won't remember

SUSAN YARBROUGH

Nan

The only one whose favorite I have been is
dying now, and I am far adrift.

Lona Cotton Futrell.
A name so right:
majestic Texas matriarch,
maiden at the hand of God,
hummer of hymns,
bather and duster in Cashmere Bouquet,
softening, softening all in her way.

She has lost one hundred pounds these last four years,
her mammary glands now shrunk to fashionable size,
her softness clinging only to her facial skin,
her body not her own.
But love for me yet sleeps intact (I know)
within her singing soul, and know also
I do that dreams in her sclerotic brain
are of this grandchild leaning, crying,
holding to her fragrant breasts as
never since the child has held.

All uncorseted she lies, averts
her blackening eyes to leak of tears,
hears me dim beside her moving bed,
moves her toothless mouth as if to say
You're mine, sweet girl,
first of six,
always first.

I tell her I am
lawyer, teacher,
woman wanting to be well and good,
remolding summer mudpies by
her roller-skating porch on which she swung
and watched, then picked me up to bathe
then feed with rice and fruits which make me
cry for her when opening their smells
to grownup me.

I say to her,
I'll break and rock and
want to die with you.
Your daughter will consume me with her
righteous daughter's grief.
I'll gag and choke on sorrow, seek
my childhood secret hiding place—
the walnut wardrobe opposite the
bed where you would hear me read
some ancient tales as I lay next to you,
your nightgown and your face cream taking up
the smell of peaches, apples, tangerines,
our favored fruits before the reading of the book.

I prayed always to die before you did.

Can I tell you how the force of you has made
the love of women midmost in my heart?

I can't, but
that is all I never told to you.

I say,
From my mother's excess and her venom

saved me you for
women's lasting love.
You make me want to heal, caress,
hold up the woman that is you in
all the women in my life.

And so I see
You're mine, sweet and soft old woman,
mine to carry in my brain and breast,
first of all,
always first.

JANINE CANAN

Once Upon a Time There Were Two Sisters

Once upon a time there were two sisters, Anna and
Suzanna. Their mother was a wicked mother and they
were sent away. Anna to one grandmother, Suzanna
across country to the other. Anna fell in love with
words, she'd send her favorites to Suzanna saying,
read this. Suzanna would read them and then she
would write. Suzanna grew up, got married and had
a daughter of her own, but one day she left her
husband, fell in love with a woman and published her
poems. Anna had always loved women, she kept her
poems quietly tucked away in the drawer, studying
them late at night, her hair was pearly gray, around
her neck she wore turquoise jewels, her voice was
as soft and deep as llama fur. Suzanna cut her hair
off so it fit like a nun's cap, white fur grew on
her face, but her manner was cold as hard-packed
snow and she grew very famous. The two sisters lived
side by side now in the same town, but even in the
same room one could see no resemblance.

Emily Dickinson Is Staying At Home

Emily Dickinson is staying at home. She's wearing
her white eyelet dress, wandering in her nightgarden,
composing a poem. Her father sleeps. Emily Dickinson
writes a letter to Mr. Higginson: Is it any good, Sir?
She laughs. She's been growing many years now, pulling
up weeds from China, sighting a lark over France,
stunned by the evening sun in her backyard as Amherst
turns past—the opal herd, the amber farm. Emily
Dickinson has a solemn face. Her eyes are very
strange. They're dark and can look inward and out.
Stars sparkle in the back of her head. In her hand,
the vermilion flower outstretched.

PAT M. KURAS

Edna St. Vincent Millay

exposing bluebeard and
echoes of daphne's footfalls
your sonnets and lines graze
on the mind's ear   gifts
of a lyrical genius like
one of sappho's own   you
know and touch the maid of
orleans, young poets and
the goddess herself   an
overwhelming spring   you
have no end   witch wife and
purple skies that fall on
lesbos   even charon cannot
steal you from us   under the
rose-pink of early morn

Daphne: a sprite, nymph, or witch in Greek mythology, who could change herself into a tree.

"Witch Wife": title of one of Millay's poems.

Charon: the ferryman who transported souls across the river Styx into Hades.

Work Poem

The little man from Dun & Bradstreet
comes into my store weekly. His suit
is gray but his eyes are magic. He comes
looking for showtunes. He gives me names,
titles, labels, even serial numbers.
I'm his pusher, supply the goods.
Last week, it was Ethel Merman, "Annie
      Get Your Gun."
Now, it's "West Side Story."
Showtunes for the Dun & Bradstreet man,
while, *what* keeps me going in my shit job?
No showtunes for me, no amusements, just
the same grimy grind, day in and
day out, all the livelong day.
No showtunes, no music, nothing
that can make me dance.

DORIS DAVENPORT

to the 'majority' from a 'minority'

i did not come by faith.
but if you must know,
i came by any means i could
& any means necessary.

i came by bus
by mastercharge
by crying and carrying on.
i came by leaning on Momma who leaned on the
lord who leaned on southern comfort
i came

in crowds
in secret code
in raging and wrath sometimes i came,
barely, and alone, now

it ain't y'r business,
how i came & i can't stand
nosey people but
this is your business:

i am not
going back.
so here i am
but what i am
ain't your business.

i have found

I have found   or

invented

a "new" language

but

don't have energy

to teach

d.s.l*

———————

*doris-as-a-second-language

SHEILAH SHOOK

Geography Lesson
Written as a birthday gift to myself

The Kara Kum desert slashes through the 38th parallel
It is not a particularly comfortable region
Colored tan, sand, beige
Arid and windy
Its landscape is a series of obstacles
and projections punctuating nothing
Stark reality in surrealism

The women on the Kara Kum are veiled and silent
Shepherds there tend flocks of the broadtailed Karakul
Sheep prized for their delicate wool
Especially that of the unborn lamb
The ewes have no horns
The gentle shepherd is also the slayer

In another part of the world
The 38th streaks through Lake Tahoe
Surrealism with no reality
The lake, a precious stone, now surrounded by
the glitter of a thousand synthetic brilliantines
Where Helen Reddy lives in solar efficient splendor
built on royalties earned singing
"I AM WOMAN, HEAR ME ROAR"

Game is shot quickly at Lake Tahoe
and seldom sees the hunter
a hundred yards downwind

The women are veiled in ice blue eyeshadow
and silent behind cocktail chatter

I have learned to fear the herder and the hunter
No matter the terrain
For they have been known to stalk
in lush subdivision valleys
and on penthouse peaks
As well as on the dry, white hot days
and in the blowing, penetrating nightwinds
on the hillsides of poverty

Where women die in tenements
Their unborn   no market value
Veiled in torn window shades
No one hears their screams
Reality is blinding, cold neon lights

As I cross my own 38th
I am developing a wariness
and the skills of evasiveness

I am strengthening my limbs
for leaping the precipices
I am keeping my horns veiled
and practicing blood cries in darkness

I no longer keep warm in Persian lamb
or consort with shepherds.

AUDREY EWART

A Vessel To Continue the Line

Wrapped in her cloth
the young girl walks toward the women she knows
made naked
she lies on the straw mat
legs open
held down
several hands holding her legs
down and wide apart
holding down her shoulders
holding down her hips
on the straw mat
under the hot sun

Seized between a thumb and two fingers
her clitoris
is hacked away
like raw meat from a chicken bone
a small dull blade, the saw
that brings the searing pain
and bloodies the place between her legs

Gut-stunned
she rises as the hands release her
fumbles her cloth around her
and walks away
fire burning between her legs

The young girl just come of age
does not cry out
she will bear the loss of blood

prolonged pain, infections
bring a high bride price to her father
bear many children to her husband
through her scar-hardened opening.

Beneath My Hands

How will you be
beneath my hands
will you be soft and firm
full and round
will you tremble
as I range over your hills
and slide into your furrows
will you open
bud by bud
or will you burst
into full flower
will your voice rise high
run deep
or purr
will you be white fire across my sky
will you be
some of these
all of these
beneath my hands

JACQUELINE LAPIDUS

Paraíbana

for C.M.R.

1. Night Journey

Already, riding north from Bahia
I dream of adventure,
the air-conditioned bus lurching over bumps
becomes a horse carrying Maria Bonita
to new exploits in Sergipe and Alagoas.
All-night cangaceiro: sweat
stains my hatband and the back of my shirt.
My lover beside me lies
awake, uneasy.   She
knows this road, the famished people
wide-eyed behind shutters,
the stifling heat.

Her father also remembers.
On a tape he sent us once, he tells
in a cracked voice how Lampião
terrorized his village when he was young.
He never saw Maria Bonita.   Now
he is gaunt and prickly as the caatinga
that grows in the sertão,
his eye tearful for the prodigal daughter
and the foreign woman she's bringing home
who wears her opinions like bullets across her chest.

2. The Welcome

The local word for us
is "flowers," & word gets around.

Neighbors craning from verandas all down the street.
Old school friends.   The phone
rings and rings, every garden in town
eager to reveal its secrets,
doctor, lawyer, Indian
chief.   Some of these ladies
hide behind their makeup,
others, even tugging children by the hand
are unmistakable.
Sueli from next door throws her arms around us,
hugs the visitor a split second
longer than is necessary.   Obsidian
eyes.   Openly outrageous, oh
I recognize this woman,
the pleasure's mine!
Two nights and many beers later,
my hand on her shoulder,
her tongue like lightning answers my questions
with a tropical storm.

3.   Exploring

In this climate, everything grows quickly:
seeds spat from a window after lunch
sprout between the flagstones in a week.
I speak the language
with a convert's passion. Sueli
attentive.   Her knee
beneath the table, warm contralto —
not in my stars for a lifetime,
simply this certainty, *won't leave here*
before I . . . you say where . . .
My lover watches,
apprehensive.

Every day we're driven to the beach,
sandy wilderness white as my European skin,
mellifluous names: Manaira, Formosa,
Cabedelo of the whaleboats,
Cabo Branco the easternmost tip
of Brazil.   Sueli's hands underwater
touch the tip of my desires,
I am burning
        don't stop.
                My lover's
watching but I've gone
too far, to the edge
of the world, to the depths of a dark
and unsuspected sea.

4.   The Excursion

Lover, the Saturday we travelled inland
to Ingá, you curious but wary
Sueli a blaze of sunlight at the wheel
her lover smiling complicity
and I enchanted,
as we strolled, tourists at the fair
among sacks of bean & manioc,
rawhide, sisal, squealing piglets,
cauldrons of feijoada,
ragged children playing in the dust,
I tried to tell you—all the way
along the cowpath where Sueli, magniloquent,
drove into a pond;
in the field where finally,
unguarded, exposed
to harsh weather and baffled interpretation
the stones of Ingá stood before us,
survivors of a past we'd seen and shared
in visions—when I saw
dancing like schoolgirl graffiti across the rockface

carvings of cunts and seven-branched candelabra,
androgynous embraces, salamanders, spirals
and symbols of the female form,
when under that pure sky I longed to open
my throat and every other orifice
to leap   to sing   to become fire
in praise of the Goddess who preserved them there,
I tried—in the profound silence
of my caring, in the still air,
in the soft burble of the brook where all of us
except you, lover, held hands
letting the current through and knowing
what we'd come for;
and huddled in the dunes
at twilight, with Sueli's songs and our own
violet shapes for warmth, I tried to tell you
while you walked away again;
and after dinner when, dizzy from cachaça
we ran so fast down the beach at Cabo Branco
two by two that in spite
of a full moon, or perhaps because, we
splashed fully dressed into the sea,
as you and Sueli's lover stumbled
giggling into each other's arms,
as Sueli embraced me openly for the first time,
as with her taste in my mouth I kissed
her lover, astonished
by her body,
delicate like you, voluptuous
like Sueli—and when you came back to me
smiling, as if the four of us
had never loved any other way but joined,
alike in our different bodies
exactly the same height—lover, I tried
to say: loving others
I am not against you

but constantly willing to love you,
loving more.

5.   The Weather Changes

next day's chill shocks
their bewildered faces blank as sky
a raw wind blowing in over Cabo Branco
deserted
we huddle round a table
red-eyed, picking
at steamed crab, not
touching

our salty clothes hang on the line
for days, refusing to dry
the pregnant cat sulks past her time
the moon like my lover's confidence
is waning

                (she has begun proceedings
                for an exit visa
                                invisible friends
                send flutesounds through the avocado trees)

feel free make/you think only of
                yourself
at home do whatever you/never ask what I
                want
it's all the same to/love stop hurting
                me

yes, but
yes, and

September: winter
of our
discontent

6. Knowing

Difficult
nights—the house double-locked,
so close
I can't breathe,
a sullen fly buzzing between twin beds.
The father drugged on TV & religion,
the mother's mealtime litany
of starches.
Across the street,
a bullfrog orchestra croaks disapproval.
I sleep lightly now,
lynx crouched among the vines at dawn
listening for the tigress,
over the wall and into her lair
before anyone's up.
I slink into my place at breakfast
smelling of jungle, sharp
as the sea-urchins we brought from the beach
one torrid morning and didn't know
how to open. *I dare.*
At the bar I devour grilled quail
bones and all,
and no amount of beer can quench my thirst.
When it rains, we wait out the clouds with ballads
—the guitar's no jealous lover.
One day Sueli asks me *will you come back?*
and I, warm & drowsy:
who knows.
    Who
knows?

7. Leaving

Sueli, wake up it's
time, it's now,

moments wrenched from packing,
goodbye to people I won't
remember,
hurry,
card in my pocket,
word in my ear,
força
calma
rode through Paraiba and seized
what we needed,
hands on fire,
Sueli

    Alone on a bus
    bound for Pernambuco and points south
    (my lover left mourning),
    alone with the new moon
    at a lunch counter in Maceió
    where the ladies' room is marked WOMEN
    & Maria Bonita dangles from souvenir keychains,
    alone between the pages of my diary
    while ballads hawked in the marketplace
    call me bandit

        Sueli, at this very moment
        you and your lover are driving
        through Amazon Valley floodwaters
        toward a new life, and I'm
        trying to make a living from my old one,
        inscribing my stones.
        In one photo you deftly decapitate a coconut,
        in another your eyes hold me
        conspirator: honor
        among thieves

cangaceiros: armed peasants who revolted against the power of the great landowners in the Northeast of Brazil. Leaders like Lampião and Maria Bonita became legendary figures.

sertão: interior of the country

caatinga: a tree

cachaça: rum

SUNITI NAMJOSHI

FEMINIST FABLES

SNOW WHITE AND ROSE GREEN

Once upon a time there were two sisters and one got married and one didn't. Or, once upon a time there were two piglets and one went to market and one didn't, or, one was straight and one wasn't. The point is, whatever they did or failed to do, they were a great disappointment to their poor mother. Luckily for them, the two sisters loved one another. When they saw that their mother was growing more and more unhappy, they proposed to her that she cut them in half and out of the two good halves make one splendid one. Their mother refused in high indignation, but she was so wretched that the dutiful daughters went to a surgeon. The surgeon obligingly sawed them in half, then interchanged halves and stuck them together. But there were still two of them. This was a problem. So they went back home and said to their mother, "Now choose the good one." But their mother was furious that they had even thought of such a scheme. "You did it to mock me," she told them angrily. "You are both bad children." When the two sisters heard her say this, the Good One wept, but the Bad One smirked.

THE BADGE-WEARING DYKE
AND HER TWO MAIDEN AUNTS

In the city of mice, which consisted entirely of mouseholes and labyrinths, two elderly spinster mice had lived together for twenty-five years. They were poor, but respectable, had once taught school, and in their small circle were generally regarded as authorities on culture. On a Friday—they distinctly remember that it was a Friday—a niece came to visit and stayed to supper. She wore no make-up—that was unexceptional—she had been to university—they believed in education—but she wore a number of badges bearing such extraordinary legends as "Gay Liberation is Our Liberation" and "Lesbians Ignite." Fortunately neither of the spinsters could read without spectacles. Nothing untoward happened till after the evening meal, and perhaps not even then. As a prelude to conversation, one of them asked, "And why do you wear those badges, my dear?" The niece replied, "To protest against the discrimination that women suffer who love one another." "Oh," said the spinster, "but we love one another, and have done so for twenty-five years." "Yes," said the niece, "but do you sleep together?" "We have shared the same bed for twenty-five years." "Well, what I mean is, do you prefer women?" "Yes, on the whole, one is so much more comfortable with one's own sex, don't you think?" The niece was nonplussed. She took off her badges and offered them to the spinsters, "Perhaps you should wear these?" But the spinsters declined, and in a curious way the niece felt glad when she wished them well and said "Good Night."

KILLER DYKE

She avoided lions. They scared her. But then she was scared of being scared. And so, when a passing lion came close to her, she stood her ground. He was magnificent. The air was charged with his male presence. The very sun had allied himself to this lord of creation. His mane shone. His sex stunned. She was afraid. Her eyes were watering. Her body trembled. But she stood where she was and tried to speak to the lion. The lion was pleased. With minimal effort he knocked her down. Then somehow she shot the lion, and was duly arrested for baiting the animals.

THE MOUSE AND THE LION

One day a lion caught a mouse, 'Spare me,' said the mouse, 'I am so little and you are so big; but, who knows, perhaps some day I will be able to do you a favour.' The lion thought this funny and let the mouse go. But a few days later the very same lion was caught in a net. After a while the mouse came along. 'Help,' called the lion, 'Help, little mouse. Chew through these ropes. Remember, after all, that you owe me a favour.' The mouse started chewing and then suddenly stopped. 'Why have you stopped?' roared the lion. 'Well, I just thought of something,' said the little mouse, 'You see, I think I have already done you a favour.' 'You haven't,' roared the lion. 'Yes, I have,' said the mouse. 'What?' roared the lion. 'Well, you see,' said the mouse, 'I haven't killed you.'

THE EXAMPLE

And the sparrows' children needed a tutor, so they hired a wren. The wren did her job conscientiously and diligently, but the sparrow parents criticized her colour, her modest exterior, and made fun of her sometimes because she wasn't married. And the sparrows' children were like any other children, wily and wilful, simple and gentle, and sometimes very kind and sometimes mean. Then, one day, there was a tremendous scandal. The birds had discovered that the wren's sexuality was not what it should be. They feared for their children. What if the wren should corrupt them morally? They summoned the wren and demanded an explanation. And the wren said, 'What is private is private, and what is public is public.' 'Oh no,' said the parents, 'We understand, you know, that you are not only a lesbian, but also a feminist, and feminists maintain that the public and private are not distinct.' 'But I don't teach sex,' said the wren, 'I teach reading and writing and simple arithmetic.' 'Ah, but what you are, after all, is something that our very own children might turn out to be. And what you are is dreadful and horrid.' 'I am not dreadful and I am not horrid,' said the wren indignantly. 'That makes it worse. You set an example,' said the parents sternly. 'So do you,' said the wren. 'Well, you're fired,' was the parents' verdict. And so the sparrows' children grew up anyhow and some were horrid, and some resisted it.

TROGLODYTE

The brutish woman lived in a cave: her hair was unkempt, her legs were hairy, and her teeth were large and strong and yellowish. She hunted for herself, and spent her spare time drawing and painting. She had ability, and her fellow cave-dwellers admired her drawings. These were chiefly of mammoth and tiger, bison and bird, and the occasional fish. Then one day she fell in love. It may not have been love, perhaps it was lust, or perhaps friendship. Whatever the exact nature of the relationship, she worked furiously. In the course of her life she drew hundreds of sketches of the other cave-woman. In time, both of them died; and in time also, the cave fell in, the tribe disappeared. By now, it is firmly established that this woman never was, that she never painted, and never lived.

Photo Credits:

Joseph Bruchac III for the photograph of Paula Gunn Allen; Tee Corinne for Martha Courtot, Caroline Overman and Jane Rule; Honey Lee Cotreell for Canyon Sam; Lindsay K. Elam for Ida VSW Red; Lisa Kanemoto for Monika Kehoe; Lynda Koolish for Elsa Gidlow; David Robinson for Mary Meigs; SRD/A. Nouri for Jacqueline Lapidus; Layle Silbert for Marilyn Hacker; Amrita Zachana for Doris Davenport.

Pamela Annas

Paula Gunn Allen

SDiane Bogus

Karen Brodine

Janine Canan

Martha Courtot

Janice Dabney

Doris Davenport

Pam Gray

Audrey Ewart

Barbara Deming in 1950

Elsa Gidlow

Jacqueline Lapidus

Marilyn Hacker

Monika Kehoe

Mary Miegs

Suniti Namjoshi

Caroline Overman

Canyon Sam

Ida VSW Red

Jane Rule

Judy Shavrien

Sheila Shook

LINDAJEAN BROWN

jazz dancin wif mama

jasmine had shorten to jazz a while ago, cut off her hair but was growin it back in braids; like cornrowed aunt sally from long years before: the kind o braids you don have to comb but once a week. had six ear holes filled wif skinny gold circles an a dot o diamond wedged in her nose. had on her good black short-sleeved shirt, an tan work pants an sandals from mexico. gotten over showin toes. in the heart pocket, was the petals from the purple iris dena give jazz to remember her by when she got on the bus. the bus was gonna take her south to monticello; makin a hundred stops from 42nd street n 8th avenue, to there. the petals shrank an squeezed perfume into her shirt an dried in the wind on the nex day o the journey.

early mornin on the bus, wif the light on the other side: jazz dozed, still, rollin her head round on her neck an catchin the air wif her open mouth. dena danced in the dream images an thru jazz blood till she waked, reachin for dena like always in the mornin, an bumped into the seat in front o her. chucklin to herself . . . "fool, you on the bus, girl."

mos people had got off in d.c. an jazz been able to stretch out in bof seats, even tho her long legs hanged over the arm o the end seat into the aisle.

jazz wushed she had some o dena's coffee right now. wushed she could see some o dena's smile—but not here, not yet or now. jazz hadn tol mama yet—one reason why she come home this time. tellin mama was right, now, but tellin this took seein mama clear in her face.

bus rolled down 95, thru towns that ain't changed since 1902. jazz seen people workin they land, cows grazin, grass growin thick an tall. jazz looked at the man's watch in the nex seat an count up the hours on her fingers. be bout 3 mo hours, then the journey be finish. least, the goin half. jazz lit up a kool an dragged on it, lettin the nicotene seep into her blood, slow, feelin the high it give her, ridin that wave.

dena had made rolls an chicken an wrapped them in foil an a paper bag for jazz to eat an not git hongry. had put 3 plums in the bag, the color o her own lips on the outside, the color o her tongue an gums on the inside. sweet, jazz thought, like the center o dena. she had one roll lef an a wing an a plum. breakfas be ok.

dus kick up so bad you couldn see nobody. mus be hot, cause it sho was dry. red clay dirt all over everywhere. jazz said out loud to no one . . .

"cain't see mama. wonder if i give her the wrong time?"

she got her suitcase with the stripe on bof sides—brown leather an yellow stripes—down from the rack over the seats.

jazz straighten her shirt an lick her dry lips. she pick up her bag, an waited her turn to file out the bus. in the sun, her eyes narrow, an the heat brought water, quick, to her forehead an under her arms. but, it loosed her body, an made walkin down the stairs an onto the groun a joy. like a fancy flight.
 . . . peoples wushin other peoples hello . . . huggin an kissin . . . some cryin, sayin how well you look, big you grown.

jazz didn see mama yet, an the peoples was clearin away. the bus had pull off like a bat out o hell, spewin all them wif red clay dirt—white man sittin in a too tight driver suit in the driver's seat, wif a sinister grin. he done reached the end o the line—carryin niggers down in the souf—an this was his home, too. so, he didn have to be nice no mo, or say yessir or ma'm to em. this prank was only the beginnin o his fun.

jazz sit on her bag, brushin off red from her pants an out her eyes. she sit in the shade o a big tree, foldin her hands, like when they use to be in sundee school. waitin for mama to come. mama was walkin, so it may have took some time.

but, then a pickup pull up, an mama got out wif her good red cotton dress on, an pretty as a young girl in her sun hat. the sun had cullered her deep coco brown, even early in june. she smiled that smile, let you know you home, an reach out her long slender arms an legs for jazz, before she got right up on her. when she did, she wrap her arms round jazz body.

"my baby! my own baby girl. don you look like water to a thirsty man to yo mama? jasmine. come here, baby. come here to mama."

an jazz bury herself in mama arms. mama busom. under mama heart. she smell an breathe everything familiar. everything she know bout herself in this life. she close her eyes.

"mama, i'm so glad you come, finely. thought i'd be sittin here into tamorrow," she teased.

"mama, i'm glad to be here. to see you agin."

aroun the laughin an rockin an swayin, the womon driver o the pickup walked. she stood behin mama, puttin her arm round her waist an pullin her kinda upright . . .

"catherine . . ."

mama straighten up an let go o jazz for a bit. she turn an smile into the womon eyes, while jazz . . . stare . . . puzzle . . . wonder.

"jasmine, meet maxine."

maxine put her hand toward jazz, who grip it firm an say hello into maxine eyes. maxine smile an say jazz look like her pictures on mama wood table, after all. she took jazz bag an put it in the back o the pickup. then, they all climb in. the truck move, wif maxine drivin, jazz in the middle, an mama by the other door.

mama talk bout jazz hair an how thin jazz was. she pat jazz heart pocket, where the purple iris petals dena give jazz was, still. they flew out in a puff on mama lap. jazz pick them up, one by one, settlin them back in her pocket.

"they pretty." mama tol her.

"a womon name dena, who is sweet to me, who is my love, mama, give em to me fo the trip. so's i could member her while i'm away."

jazz confessed.

"maxine an me been together more'n a year now. since close after the las time i seen you in the flesh, jasmine. she good to me an love me. an i love her," mama began.

"they's limonade an ginger bread at home. we can all sit out on the po'ch an have a long talk, girl. they's always mo news than you kin put in a letter."

BETH BRANT

A SIMPLE ACT

for Denise Dorsz

Gourds climbing the fence. Against the rusted criss-cross wires, the leaves are fresh. The green, ruffled plants twine around the wooden posts that need painting. The fruit of the vine hangs in irregular shapes. Some are smooth. Others bumpy and scarred. All are colors of the earth. Brown. Green. Gold.

A gourd is a hollowed-out shell, used as a utensil. I imagine women together, sitting outside the tipis and lodges, carving and scooping. Creating bowls for food. Spoons for drinking water. A simple act, requiring lifetimes to learn. At times the pods were dried and rattles made to amuse babies. Or noisemakers, to call the spirits in sorrow and celebration.

I am taking a break from my hot room; from the writing, where I dredge for ghosts. The writing that unearths pain, old memories.

I cover myself with paper, the ink making tracks; like animals who follow the scent of water past familiar ground.

I invent new from the old.

STORY ONE

Sandra . . . In the third, fourth, and fifth grades, we were best friends. Spending nights at each others' houses, our girl bodies hugging tight. We had much in common. Our families were large and sloppy. We occupied places of honor due to our fair skin and hair. Assimilation separating us from our ancient and inherited place of home. Your Russian gave way to English. Your blonde hair and freckles a counterpoint to the darkness of eye and black hair massed and trembling around your mother's head. My blonde hair, fine and thin, my skin pink and flushed in opposition to the sleek, black hair of my aunts, my uncle, my father. Their eyes dark, hidden by folds of skin. Anachronisms . . . except to each other. Our friendship fit us well.

We invented stories about ourselves. We were children from another planet. We were girls from an undiscovered country. We were alien beings in families that were "different." Different among the different. We were the hopes of all.

Your big sister, Olga, wore falsies. We stole a pair from her and took turns tucking them inside our undershirts. We pretended to be big girls, kissing on the lips and touching our foam rubber breasts. Imagining what being grown meant. In the sixth and seventh grades, our blood started to flow, our breasts turned into a reality of sweet flesh and waiting nipples. The place between our thighs filled with a wanting so tender, an intensity of heat from which our fingers emerged, shimmering with liquid energy, our bodies spent with the expression of our growing strength. When we began to know what this was, that it was called love . . . someone told on us. Told on us. Through my bedroom window where we lay on the bed, listening to the radio, stroking blonde hair . . . Roger, the boy next door, saw us and told on us. Our mothers were properly upset. We heard the words from them . . . You can't play with each other anymore . . . You should be ashamed . . . WHAT WILL PEOPLE THINK?

We fought in our separate ways. You . . . screaming in Russian as your father hit you with his belt. Cursing him. Vowing revenge. Your mother stood painfully watching, but did not interfere, upholding the morality of the family. My mother shamed me by promising not to tell the rest of the family. I refused to speak to her for weeks, taking refuge in silence, the acceptable solution. I hated her for the complicity we shared.

Sandra . . . we couldn't help seeing each other. You lived across the street. We'd catch glimpses of the other running to school. Our eyes averted, never focusing. The belt marks, the silences, the shame, restoring us once again, to our rightful places. We were good girls, nice girls, after all. So like an old blouse that had become too thin and frayed, an embarrassment to wear, our friendship was put away, locked up inside our past. Entering the eighth grade in 1954, we were thirteen years old. Something hard, yet invisible, had formed a thick shell over our memory. We went the way of boys, backseats of cars, self-destruction. I heard you were put in the hospital with sugar diabetes. I sent a card . . . unsigned. Your family eventually moved away. I never saw you again. Sandra . . . we are forty-one now . . . I have three daughters . . . a woman lover . . . I am a writer.

Sandra . . . I am remembering our losses.

Sandra . . . I am remembering . . . I loved you.

CHAPTER ONE

We have a basket filled with gourds. It is woven from sweet-grass and the scent stirs up the air and lights on our skin. This still-life sits on a table in front of our bedroom window. In late afternoon, the sun glances around the hanging plants, printing designs on the wall, and on our arms as we lay on our bed. We trust our love to each others' care. The room grows dusky and heavy with words. Our lungs expand to breathe the life gestating in the space connecting your eyes to mine. You put your hand on my face and imprint forever in memory, this passage of love and faith. As I watch you come from your bath, I am infused with love and feeling. As you raise your arms to dry your hair, I reach to touch that curve of flesh coursing with blood . . . with life. I pull you towards me, my hands soothed by the wetness on your back and between your thighs. You smell of cinnamon and clean water. Desire shapes us. Desire to touch one another with our hands, our eyes, our mouths, our minds. I bend over you, kissing the hollow in your throat . . . the pulse leaping under my lips.

We touch . . . dancers wearing shells of turtles, feathers of eagles, bones of our people. We touch.

STORY TWO

The house I grew up in was a small, frame box. It had two stories. My sister, cousins and I shared a room on the second floor. A chestnut tree rubbed its branches against our window. In the summer, we opened the glass panes and coaxed the arms of the tree into the room. Grandpa spoke to the tree every night. We listened to the words, holding our breath and our questions in fear of breaking a magic we knew was happening, but couldn't name.
Summer . . . 1954.

In our house, we spoke the language of censure. Sentences stopped in the middle. The joke without a punch line. Chopped-off words before the meanings became clear. The mixture of a supposed-to-be-forgotten Mohawk, strangled with uneasy English.

I was a dreamer. Somewhere in the wishfulness of my mind, places of freedom were being created. Words that my family whispered in their sleep, could be shouted. Words that we were not supposed to say, could be sung out loud; like the hymns Grandma sang on Sundays. The secrets we held to ourselves. We swallowed them. They lay at the bottoms of our stomachs, making us fat with nerves and itching from inside.

The secrets we held to ourselves.

The secret that my mom's father refused to see her after she married a dark man . . . an Indian man.

The secret that my uncle drank himself to oblivion most weekends when he couldn't hitch a ride home to the rez, eight hours away. The secret that Grandma didn't go out much because a storekeeper called her a name and wouldn't wait on her.

The secret that Grandpa carried a heart inside him clogged with the starches, the fats, the poverty of food that as a young boy, as an Indian, he had no choice about eating.

All of us, weighted down by invisible scales. Balancing always, our life among the assimilators, and our life of memory.

And always, always, the faint tinge of shame, no matter how well we tried to accommodate . . . to fit in.

I had learned the lessons. I was a clever girl, quick to know. I kept my mouth shut. I kept the quiet.

One night in August, a fire in the basement.

Things burned.

Secret things.

Indian things.

Things the neighbors never saw.

False Faces . . . Beaded necklaces . . . Moccasins . . . Old letters written in Mohawk . . .

Turtle rattles . . . Corn husks.

Secrets brought from home.

Secrets protecting us in hostile places.

Did you lose anything? The neighbors stood, anxious to not know. The night air was still. It was hot. The moon hung full and white. The stars in a crazy design over us.

I looked for Sandra. Across the street, her face caught like a photograph in the window of her flat. We stared.

Did you lose anything? The question came again.

Just a few old things . . . and Grandma and Grandpa stepped into the house, led by my mother's and father's hands. My Grandparents tears were acid, tunneling holes in their cheeks.

Don't forget this night, kondirio. Don't forget this night.

Grandfather looked at me . . . the phrase repeated again and again . . .

Don't forget this night.

Grandfather's back became a little more stooped. Every day he looked a little more Indian. He lapsed into Mohawk at odd moments. His heart stopped in his sleep . . . heavy . . . constricted . . . silenced.

Grandmother's back became a little thicker. Her shoulders were two eagles transfixed on a mountain, checked in flight. Her hands grew large and knobby from arthritis. Still, she made the fry bread, the corn soup, the quilts, the jams, and changed the diapers of her great-grandchildren.

She never spoke of that night. She continued to sing the hymns, her eyes fading, watery with age. She died . . . her heart quitting in her sleep.

Summer, 1954.

I closed the windows and covered my ears to the knocking of the tree.

CHAPTER TWO

In my room overlooking the back yard. Through the open window, I smell the cut grass, hear the vines on the fence make a whispery sound. The gourds rattle as a breeze moves along quickly, carrying a promise of autumn and change. I sit at the desk, pen in my hand, paper scattered underneath; trying to bring forth sound and words.

Unblocking my throat . . . Untying my tongue . . . Scraping sand out of my eyes . . . Pulling each finger out of the fist I have carried at my side . . . Unclenching my teeth . . . Burning the brush ahead of me, brambles cutting across my mind.

Each memory a pain in the heart, but *this* heart keeps pumping blood through my body, keeping me alive.

I write because to not write is a breach of faith.

Out of a past where amnesia was the expected . . . Out of a past occupied with quiet . . . Out of a past, I make truth for a future.

Cultures betrayed by assimilation.

Cultures gone up in flames.

The smell of burning leather, paper, flesh; filling the spaces where memory fails.

The smell of a chestnut tree, its leaves making magic.

The smell of Sandra's hair, like dark coffee and incense, as we touched in pleasure.

I close my eyes at my desk. Pictures rapidly unreeling on my eyelids. Portraits of beloved people flashing by so quickly.

Opening my eyes, I think of the seemingly ordinary things that women do, and how, with the brush of an eyelash against a cheek, an electric pulse in the brain, the movement of pencil on paper, power is born.

A gourd is hollowed-out shell, used as a utensil.

We make our bowls from the stuff of nature. Of life.

We carve and scoop, discarding the pulp.

Ink on paper, picking up the trail I left so many lives ago.

Leaving my mark, my footprints, my sign.

I write what I know.

PAULA GUNN ALLEN

IN THE SHADOWS SINGING
SHE REMEMBERED*

It had been the apple tree. The long spring days there. With the girl. They had watched the village going. They had watched the clouds. When they thirsted they climbed down from the branches and walked to the nearby spring. Took a long sweet drink.

Elena had taught Ephanie about the weeds. Which to eat. When they had gathered prickly pears in the summer, brushing carefully the tiny spines from the fruit before they ate. They had wandered the mesas and climbed the nearer peaks. Together they had dreamed. Sharing. They never talked about growing up. What that would mean.

They had ridden horses. Pretended to be ranchers. Chased the village cattle around the town. Suffered scoldings for it. Learned to be trick riders. Roy Rogers and Hopalong Cassidy. Maybe they could be stunt men in Hollywood if they got good enough at it. If they could learn to jump from the rooftop onto the horse's back. They had chased the clouds.

Or lying, dreaming, had watched them, tracing faces and glorious beast shapes in the piling, billowing thunderheads. On July mornings they had gone out from their separate homes, laughing, feet bare and joyful in the road's early dust. The early wind cool and fresh, the bright sunlight making promises it would never keep. They had lain together in the alfalfa field of Elena's father, quiet, at peace.

They were children and there was much they did not know.

In their seasons they grew. Walking the road between their houses, lying languorous and innocent in the blooming boughs

---

*An excerpt from the novel *The Women Who Owned the Shadows* (San Francisco: Spinsters, Ink, 1983).

of the apple tree. Amid the fruiting limbs. And had known themselves and their surroundings in terms of each other's eyes. Though their lives were very different, their identity was such that the differences were never strange. They had secret names for each other, half joking, half descriptive, Snow White and Rose Red, they named themselves, in recognition of the fairness of Elena, the duskyness of Ephanie. In recognition also of the closeness they shared, those friends.

The events that measured their shared lives were counted in the places that they roamed, and Ephanie always remembered her childhood that way. The river, the waterfall, the graveyard, the valley, the mesas, the peaks. Each crevice they leaped over. Each danger they challenged, each stone, each blade of grass. A particularity that would shape her life.

They had especially loved the shadows. Where they grew, lavender, violet, purple, or where those shadows would recede. On the mountain slopes and closer by, beneath the shading trees. And the blue enfolding distance surrounding that meant the farthest peaks. Shared with them in their eyes, in their stories, but where, together, they had never been.

In all those years, in spite of distance, in spite of difference, in spite of change, they understood the exact measure of their relationship, the twining, the twinning. There were photographs of them from that time. Because Elena's gold-tinged hair looked dark in the photograph's light, no one could say which was Elena, which Ephanie. With each other they were each one doubled. They were thus complete.

Jump.

Fall.

Remember you are flying. Say you are a bird.

She had said that, Ephanie. Had urged Elena to leap the great crevices between the huge sandstone formations that shaped the mesas they roamed. Some of the leaps were wide and the ground far below. She had always done the leading. Elena, devoted, did what Ephanie decided. Or it seemed that way.

Ephanie didn't want to remember it that way. Wanted the fact to be that Elena had gone on her own windings, ones not of Ephanie's making. And in some cases, that was true. There were some things that no matter how Ephanie urged them, Elena would not do. Some ways in which she remained safe within her own keeping. Sometimes, when she had adamantly refused, Ephanie would give up and go back to her own home. And it also went, some times, the other way.

They did not argue. They did not fight. Elena would do what was of her own wanting. And while it seemed that the dark girl was leading, the fair one did the guiding. And in her quiet, un-argumentative, unobtrusive way, she kept them both safe within the limits of their youthful abilities, gave the lessons and boundaries that encompassed their lives.

Kept them safe. Or almost so. Except for that one time that she hadn't. Kept them safe. Had missed some signal. Had turned aside in some way, away or toward, a split second too soon, too late. Had not known in time not to speak. Had not known what her words, in time, in consequence, would create.

Perhaps it had been the shadows that betrayed her. The certain angle of light that somehow disoriented her. Perhaps so accustomed to being safe, she did not know the danger, any danger that might tear the web of their being. Shredding. Shattering. Splintering.

Or maybe it was the sun. The bright, the pitiless, the unwavering sun.

But whatever had disturbed her knowing, her keeping in time with the turns and twists of their sharing, their lives, in that splitting second everyone had abandoned Ephanie. Everything had gone away.

THEY WENT ON A SHORT JOURNEY

It was on a certain day. They went hiking. Exploring. They went walking. It was an adventure. One they had planned for a long time. Ever since they were small. They planned to walk to Picacho. The peak. That rose, igneous formation, straight up from the surrounding plain. The arid floor of the semi-desert of their homeland.

They wanted to climb the peak. To go to the top. To see. Elena said you could see the next village. The one that was invisible from where they lived. She told Ephanie the story, one she had recounted before. Much of what Ephanie knew about the people and land around them she learned from Elena. She didn't hear much that others told her. Not for many years.

Not that others had not spoken. Had not told her stories, had not given ideas, opinions, methods. They had. Some part of Ephanie recorded what they told her. What they said. But she did not acknowledge it until later. Not for many years. She did not understand how that had happened. But it did.

They had planned in the last days before their journey very well. Deciding what to take. What would not be too heavy to carry. What would not get in their way. What to wear, for comfort and protection, in the heat, against the stone. Which shirts, which length pants, which shoes. They knew they would get thirsty. It was July.

They wore tennis shoes and jeans. Usually they went barefoot from spring well into fall. Every chance they got. But this journey was special. It signified accomplishing. That they were grown. That they knew something, could put it into use.

They took oranges. For the juice. They knew how to use them, slit the rind with a toughened thumbnail, in a circle. Peel the small circle of rind away from the flesh. Press finger into the fruit, firmly, gently. So as not to lose too much juice. The juice was precious. It would sustain them. Then put the opening thus made to their mouths. Sucking. When all the juice was thus taken, they would split open the fruit and eat the pulp. And the white furry lining of the rind. Elena said it was sweet. That it was healthy.

Ephanie never ate an orange that way later. It didn't seem right. She didn't know why she wouldn't. Like her dislike of spiders. Which made no sense either. She remembered how it had gone, that journey, and why they had learned to eat oranges that particular way. She didn't understand her unwillingness to follow that childhood ritual. Not for a long time. And she found the lining bitter. Peeled it carefully away from the fruit all of her adult life. Threw it away.

But she loved the smell of oranges. The orange oil that clung to her hands when she was done. Its fragrance. Its echoing almost remembered pain. She would sniff it, dreaming, empty in thought, empty in mind, on her way to the faucet to wash it off her hands. And in the flood of water and soap she would banish what she did not know. Averting. Avoiding. Voiding. Pain.

They met in the early morning. While the cool wind blew down from the mountain. The way they were going was into the wind. The earth sparkled. The leaves. The sun was just getting started. Like a light from elsewhere it touched their eyes, their hands. They shivered slightly, shaking. They began to walk. Taking the road that curved upward. Upward and out. They were leaving. They knew that. They knew they would never return.

They didn't talk about that intuition, but walked, silent, amiable, close. They listened to the soft padding of their footfall on the dusty road, watched their shadows move, silent, alongside of them. Elena told Ephanie how high the peak was. Much taller than it looked. They speculated about climbing it. Ephanie was afraid of heights that had no branches to hold on to, but she never let on. She had never let on.

The great isolate rock rose maybe a hundred feet from the ground. Its top was slender, precarious. It stood alone, gray and silent, reaching into the sky. It was a proud rock. A formation. It brooded there on the plain between the villages. It guarded the road to the mountain. Sentinel.

The story it bore was an old one. Familiar. Everywhere. They remembered the old tale as they watched the rock grow larger, approaching it. About the woman who had a lover. Who had died in a war. She was pregnant. Lonely, desperate, she went to Picacho, climbed to the top, jumped to her death. That was one version, the one Elena's Chicano people told.

There was another version, one that Ephanie's Guadalupe people told. The woman was in love with a youth she was forbidden to marry. He was a stranger, and she had fallen in love with him somehow. Maybe he was a Navajo. Maybe he was a Ute. But her love was hopeless from the start. Then the people found out that she was seeing the youth secretly. They were very angry. They scolded her. Said the things that would happen to the people because of her actions. Shamed her. Hurt and angry, she had gone to Picacho. Climbed to the top. Jumped to her death.

Ephanie imagined that climb. The woman finding places to put her hands. Her feet. Tentative, climbing. Tentative but sure. Shaking. She climbed to the place where the rock was narrowest. Where the drop was straight and steep. Dizzy she had stood there, thinking perhaps of her anguish, of her rage, of her grief. Wondering, maybe, if whether what she contemplated was wise. No one knew what she had been thinking. They must have wondered about it. They must have told themselves stories about what had gone through her mind as she stood, wavering, just on the edge of the narrow rock bridge that connected the two slightly taller peaks of the formation.

From there she could have seen the wide sweep of the land, barren, hungry, powerful as it raised itself slow and serene toward the lower slopes of the mountains to the north beyond Picacho and was there lost to the wilderness of tabletop hills, soaring slopes, green grasses, flowers, shadows, springs, cliffs, and above them the treeless towering peak. Where it became wilderness. Where it came home.

She could have seen that, looking northward. Where the mountain called Ts'pin'a, Woman Veiled in Clouds, waited, brooding, majestic, almost monstrously powerful. Or she could look southward, eastward, toward the lands the people tended, that held and nurtured them. But probably she had not looked outward. Had not seen the sky, the piling, moving thunderheads. The gold in them. The purpling blue. The dazzling, eye-splitting white. The bellies of them pregnant, ripe with rain about to be born. The living promise of their towering strength. For if she had seen them, would she have jumped?

THEY MAKE THE CLIMB

By the time they got to the foot of the peak it was late morning. The sun was high and the earth around them looked flat. Sunbitten. The shadows had retreated to cooler places for the long day. Ephanie, slender, sturdy, brown, and Elena, slender, sturdy, hair tinged with gold, lightly olive skin deepened almost brown by the summer sun, sat down to rest amid the gray boulders that lay in piles at the base of the peak. They ate their oranges. Looked at the climb that faced them, uneasy. The gray rock soared above their heads, almost smooth. Ephanie looked at Elena for reassurance, thinking how beautiful her friend was, sweating, laughing. Wanted to reach out and touch her face. To hold her hand, brown and sturdy like her own. Reached and touched the smooth brown skin, brushed tenderly back the gold-streaked hair.

"When we get home," she said, "let's go to the apple tree and cool off."

"I can't," Elena said. "I have to go with my mother to town. We're going to stay a few days at my sister's." She looked away from Ephanie. Looked at the ground. Ephanie felt uneasiness crawling around in her stomach. She shifted her weight away from Elena. She didn't know why she felt that way. "Let's go on up," she said.

They climbed. Elena went first. Finding places to put hands and feet. They pretended they were mountains, climbing Mt. Everest. They didn't have ropes, but they knew about testing rock and brush before trusting weight to them. They climbed over the boulders and up the first stage of the climb. That part was fairly easy. It was steep, but there was a broad abutment that circled most of the peak, as though supporting its slender, massive skyward thrust. The abutment was hard packed dirt, light sandstone and the gray rock, probably volcanic, that formed Picacho.

They came to a resting place, high above the valley floor. It was very hot. They sat and looked around them. The rest of the peak rose above them along a narrow path that rose toward it from where they sat. A sheer drop on either side. Dizzy. Can we cross that. They looked into each other's eyes. Daring. Testing. Their old familiar way. "I don't think I can get across that. It makes me dizzy," Ephanie said. Elena said, since Ephanie had admitted her fear, "Just crawl across it. That's what I'm going to do. I'm not going to try and walk across. We can crawl. It's not far." And she began crawling across the smooth sand that lay over the rock bridge that stretched between them and the smooth curving roundness of the farther peak. "Look down," Elena said. "It's really far."

Ephanie, on hands and knees, crept behind Elena. Feeling foolish, scared. Foolish in her fearfulness. Shaking. She did look down. It was a long way to the ground. She imagined falling. Smashing herself on the rocks below. How Elena would manage. Going home to tell them she had fallen. How the woman long ago had fallen. From here.

They got across the narrow bridge and stood up, clinging to the gray rock of the highest point that rose some three feet above their feet. They climbed up on it, scooting their bodies up and then turning to lie stomach-down on the flat peak. They looked down, over the back side of the peak. Saw the mountain a few miles beyond. "Let's stand up," one of them said. They stood, trembling slightly, and looked around. They saw the villages, one north of them, the other, just beyond it to the west.

They rested for a while, wishing they hadn't left the rest of the oranges down below. They realized they still had to climb back down—the part they were always forgetting. As they examined the descent, Elena said, "Ephanie there's something I have to tell you." She didn't look at her friend. She looked at her hands. Sweating and lightly streaked where the sweat had washed some of the dust of their climb away. "I can't come over to your place any more."

The sun was blazing down on them, unconcerned. It was so hot. Ephanie looked at Elena's hands intently. She didn't speak for a long time. She couldn't swallow. She couldn't breathe. For some reason her chest hurt. Aching. She didn't know why. Anything.

She tried to think, to understand. They had been together all their lives. What did Elena mean. She wondered if it was because she had more. Of everything. Dresses, boarding school, a bigger house. A store-owner for a father. A trader.

Elena's father had a small cantina that he owned. But he didn't make a lot of money at it. He drove a school bus, to make ends meet.

Elena's house had three rooms. Besides the kitchen. They were all used for sleeping. One of them they used as a living room too. One of them was very small, hardly large enough for the tiny iron bedstead it held. Five or six people lived there, depending on whether her brothers were both there or not. They didn't have running water, and their toilet was outdoors. Ephanie thought maybe that was what was the matter. That they were growing up. That now that they were nearing adulthood, such things mattered. Were seen in some way that caused anger, caused shame.

When Ephanie didn't say anything for so long, Elena said, "It's because my mother thinks we spend too much time with each other." She looked at Ephanie, eyes shut against her. Not closed, open, but nothing of herself coming through them. Nothing in them taking her in. Ephanie sat, thinking she was dreaming. This didn't make any sense. What could be wrong? What could be happening. How could she not see Elena? Be with her? Who would she be with then, if not Elena?

She put out her hand. Took hold of Elena's arm. Held it, tightly. Swaying. She looked over the side of the peak. Thought about flying. Dropping off. She thought of going to sleep.

She moved so that she could put her hand on Elena's arm. Held her like that, staring. Trying to speak. Not being able to. There were no words. Only too many thoughts, feelings, churning in her like the whirlwind, *chinde*, dustdevils on the valley floor below. "What are you talking about," she finally said. Her voice sounded strange in her ears.

Elena tried to back away, get loose from Ephanie's hand. Pulled away, but not completely. She looked at Ephanie. Her face was wet. Beads of sweat had formed along her upper lip. She wiped them away with the back of her hand. Her eyes looked flat, gave off no light. Her light brown eyes that were flecked with gold. Her brown face had a few freckles scattered over it. They stood out now, sharp.

"You know," she said, her voice low. "The way we've been lately. Hugging and giggling. You know." She looked down at her hands, twisting against themselves in her lap. "I asked the sister about that, after school. She said it was the devil. That I mustn't do anything like that. That it was a sin. And she told my mother. She says I can't come over any more."

Ephanie sat. Stunned. Mind empty. Stomach a cold cold stone. The hot sun blazed on her head. She felt sick. She felt herself shrinking within. Understood, wordlessly, exactly what Elena was saying. How she could understand what Ephanie had not understood. That they were becoming lovers. That they were in love. That their loving had to stop. To end. That she was falling. Had fallen. Would not recover from the fall, smashing, the rocks. That they were in her, not on the ground.

She finally remembered to take her hand off of Elena's arm. To put it in her pocket. She stood up again. Almost lost her balance. How will we ever get down, she wondered. She couldn't see very well. She realized her eyes were blurred with tears. "Why did you do that," she said. "How could you tell anyone? How did you know, what made you ask? Why didn't you ask me?" And realized the futility of her words. The enormity of the abyss she was falling into. The endless, endless depth of the void.

"I was scared. I thought it was wrong. It is." Elena looked at Ephanie, eyes defiant, flat and hard, closed.

"Then why did we come today? Why get me all the way up here and then tell me?" Ephanie felt her face begin to crumble, to give way. Like the arroyo bank gave way in the summer rains. She didn't want Elena to see her like that, giving in to anguish, to weakness, to tears.

"I'm sorry." That was all Elena would say.

They got down from the peak the way they had come, using lifelong habits of caution and practice to guide them. In silence they walked the long way back to the village. Elena went inside when they came to her house. Ephanie went the rest of the way, not so far however long it seemed, alone. She went to the apple tree and climbed up into it. Hid her face in the leaves. She sat there, hiding, for a very long time.

HENRY HANDEL RICHARDSON

TWO HANGED WOMEN

Hand in hand the youthful lovers sauntered along the esplanade. It was a night in midsummer; a wispy moon had set, and the stars glittered. The dark mass of the sea, at flood, lay tranquil, slothfully lapping the shingle.

"Come on, let's make for the usual," said the boy.

But on nearing their favourite seat they found it occupied. In the velvety shade of the overhanging sea-wall, the outlines of two figures were visible.

"Oh, blast!" said the lad. "That's torn it. What now, Baby?"

"Why. let's stop here, Pincher, right close up, till we frighten 'em off."

And very soon loud, smacking kisses, amatory pinches and ticklings, and skittish squeals of pleasure did their work. Silently the intruders rose and moved away.

But the boy stood gaping after them, open-mouthed.

"Well, I'm *damned!* If it wasn't just two hanged women!"

Retreating before a salvo of derisive laughter, the elder of the girls said: "We'll go out on the breakwater." She was tall and thin, and walked with a long stride.

Her companion, shorter than she by a bobbed head of straight flaxen hair, was hard put to it to keep pace. As she pegged along she said doubtfully, as if in self-excuse: "Though I really ought to go home. It's getting late. Mother will be angry."

They walked with finger-tips lightly in contact; and at her words she felt what was like an attempt to get free, on the part of the fingers crooked in hers. But she was prepared for this, and held fast, gradually working her own up till she had a good half of the other hand in her grip.

For a moment neither spoke. Then, in a low, muffled voice,

came the question: "Was she angry last night, too?"

The little fair girl's reply had an unlooked-for vehemence. "You know she wasn't!" And, mildly despairing: "But you never *will* understand. Oh, what's the good of . . . of anything!"

And on sitting down she let the prisoned hand go, even putting it from her with a kind of push. There it lay, palm upwards, the fingers still curved from her hold, looking like a thing with a separate life of its own; but a life that was ebbing.

On this remote set, with their backs turned on lovers, lights, the town, the two girls sat and gazed wordlessly at the dark sea, over which great Jupiter was flinging a thin gold line. There was no sound but the lapping, sucking, sighing, of the ripples at the edge of the breakwater, and the occasional screech of an owl in the tall trees on the hillside.

But after a time, having stolen more than one side-glance at her companion, the younger seemed to take heart of grace. With a childish toss of the head that set her loose hair swaying, she said, in a tone of meaning emphasis: "I like Fred."

The only answer was a faint, contemptuous shrug.

"I tell you I *like* him!"

"Fred? Rats!"

"No it isn't . . . that's just where you're wrong, Betty. But you think you're so wise. Always."

"I know what I know."

"Or imagine you do! But it doesn't matter. Nothing you can say makes any difference. I like him, and always shall. In heaps of ways. He's so big and strong, for one thing: it gives you such a safe sort of feeling to be with him . . . as if nothing could happen while you were. Yes, it's . . . it's . . . well, I can't help it, Betty, there's something *comfy* in having a boy to go about with—like other girls do. One they'd eat their hats to get, too! I can see it in their eyes when we pass; Fred with his great long legs and broad shoulders—I don't nearly come up to them—and his blue eyes with the black lashes, and his shiny black hair. And I like his tweeds, the Harris smell of them, and his dirty old pipe, and the way he shows his teeth—he's got *topping* teeth—when he laughs and says 'ra-*ther!*' And other people, when they see us, look . . . well I don't quite know how to say it, but they look sort of pleased; and they make room for us and let us into the dark corner-seats at the pictures, just as if we'd a right to them. And they never laugh. (Oh, I can't *stick* being laughed at!—and that's the truth.) Yes, it's so comfy, Betty darling . . . such a warm cosy comfy feeling. Oh, *won't* you understand?"

"Gawd! why not make a song of it?" But a moment later, very fiercely: "And who is it's taught you to think all this? Who's hinted it and suggested it till you've come to believe it? . . . believe it's what you really feel."

"She hasn't! Mother's never said a word . . . about Fred."

"Words?—why waste words? . . . when she can do it with a cock of the eye. For your Fred, that!" and the girl called Betty held her fingers aloft and snapped them viciously. "But your mother's a different proposition."

"I think you're simply horrid."

To this there was no reply.

"*Why* have you such a down on her? What's she ever done to you? . . . except not get ratty when I stay out late with Fred. And I don't see how you can expect . . . being what she is . . . and with nobody but me—after all she *is* my mother . . . you can't alter that. I know very well—and you know, too—I'm not *too* putrid-looking. But"—beseechingly—"I'm *nearly* twenty-five now, Betty. And other girls . . . well, she sees them, every one of them, with a boy of their own, even though they're ugly, or fat, or have legs like sausages—they've only got to ogle them a bit—the girls, I mean . . . and there they are. And Fred's a good sort—he is, really!—and he dances well, and doesn't drink, and so . . . so why *shouldn't* I like him? . . . and off my own bat . . . without it having to be all Mother's fault, and me nothing but a parrot, and without any will of my own?"

"Why? Because I know her too well, my child! I can read her as you'd never dare to . . . even if you could. She's sly, your mother is, so sly there's no coming to grips with her . . . one might as well try to fill one's hand with cobwebs. But she's got a hold on you, a stranglehold, that nothing'll loosen. Oh! mothers aren't fair—I mean it's not fair of nature to weigh us down with them and yet expect us to be our own true selves. The handicap's too great. All those months, when the same blood's running through two sets of veins—there's no getting away from that, ever after. Take yours. As I say, does she need to open her mouth? Not she! She's only got to let it hang at the corners, and you reek, you drip with guilt."

Something in these words seemed to sting the younger girl. She hit back. "I know what it is, you're jealous, that's what you are! . . . and you've no other way of letting it out. But I tell you this. If ever I marry—yes *marry!*—it'll be to please myself, and nobody else. Can you imagine me doing it to oblige her?"

Again silence.

"If I only think what it would be like to be fixed up and settled, and able to live in peace, without this eternal dragging two ways . . . just as if I was being torn in half. And see Mother smiling and happy again, like she used to be. Between the two of you I'm nothing but a punch-ball. Oh, I'm fed up with it! . . . fed up to the neck. As for you . . . And yet you can sit there as if you were made of stone! Why don't you *say* something? *Betty!* Why won't you speak?"

But no words came.

"I can *feel* you sneering. And when you sneer I hate you more than any one on earth. If only I'd never seen you!"

"Marry your Fred, and you'll never need to again."

"I will, too! I'll marry him, and have a proper wedding like other girls, with a veil and bridesmaids and bushels of flowers. And I'll live in a house of my own, where I can do as I like, and be left in peace, and there'll be no one to badger and bully me—Fred wouldn't . . . ever! Besides, he'll be away all day. And when he came back at night, he'd . . . I'd . . . I mean I'd—" But here the flying words gave out; there came a stormy breath and a cry of: "Oh, Betty, Betty! . . . I couldn't, no, I couldn't! It's when I think of *that* . . . Yes, it's quite true! I like him all right, I do indeed, but only as long as he doesn't come too near. If he even sits too close, I have to screw myself up to bear it"—and flinging herself down over her companion's lap, she hid her face. "And if he tries to touch me, Betty, or even takes my arm or puts his round me . . . And then his face . . . when it looks like it does sometimes . . . all wrong . . . as if it had gone all wrong—oh! then I feel I shall have to scream—out loud. I'm afraid of him . . . when he looks like that. Once . . . when he kissed me . . . I could have died with the horror of it. His breath . . . his breath . . . and his mouth—like fruit pulp—and the black hairs on his wrists . . . and the way he looked—and . . . and everything! No. I can't, I can't . . . nothing will make me . . . I'd rather die twice over. But what am I to do? Mother'll *never* understand. Oh, why has it got to be like this? I want to be happy, too . . . and everything's all wrong. You tell me, Betty darling, you help me, you're older . . . you *know* . . . and you can help me, if you will . . . if you only will!" And locking her arms round her friend she drove her face deeper into the warmth and darkness, as if, from the very fervour of her clasp, she could draw the aid and strength she needed.

Betty had sat silent, unyielding, her sole movement being to loosen her own arms from her sides and point her elbows outwards, to hinder them touching the arms that lay round her. But at this last appeal she melted; and gathering the young girl to her breast, she held her fast.—And so for long she continued to sit, her chin resting lightly on the fair hair, that was silky and downy as an infant's, and gazing with sombre eyes over the stealthily heaving sea.

RENEE VIVIEN

PRINCE CHARMING*

"told by Gesa Karoly"

I promised you, my curious little girl, to tell you the true story of Sarolta Andrassy. You knew her, didn't you? You remember her black hair with blue and red highlights, and her eyes like a lover's —begging and melancholy.

Sarolta Andrassy lived in the country with her old mother. For neighbors she had the Szecheny family, who had just left Budapest forever. Really, they were a bizarre family! It was easy to mistake Bela Szecheny for a little girl, and his sister, Terka, for a little boy. Curiously enough, Bela possessed all the feminine virtues and Terka, all the masculine faults. Bela's hair was a copper blond; Terka's was a livelier, rather reddish blond. The brother and sister strangely resembled each other—and that's very rare among members of the same family, no matter what they say.

Bela's mother was not yet resigned to cutting off the beautiful blond curls of the little boy or to exchanging his graceful muslin or velvet skirts for vulgar pants. She coddled him like a little girl. As for Terka, she kept shooting up, like a wild weed. . . . She lived outdoors, climbing on the trees, marauding, robbing the kitchen gardens. She was unbearable and at war with the world. She was a child who was neither tender nor communicative. Bela, on the other hand, was gentleness itself. He showed his adoration for his mother by making much of her and by caressing her. Terka loved no one, and no one loved her.

Sarolta came one day to visit the Szecheny family. Her loving eyes in her thin, pale face seemed to be begging. Bela greatly

---

*Translated by Karla Jay and Yvonne M. Klein

pleased her, and they played together a great deal. Looking wild, Terka prowled around them. When Sarolta spoke to her, she fled.

She could have been pretty, this incomprehensible Terka. . . . But she was too tall for her age, too thin, too awkward, too ungainly, whereas Bela was so dainty and so sweet! . . .

Several months later, the Szecheny family left Hungary. Bela had an excessively delicate chest, being in general rather frail. On the advice of the doctor, his mother took him to Nice, along with his recalcitrant little sister. Sarolta cried bitterly over losing her playmate.

In her dreams, Sarolta always evoked the too frail and too pretty little boy whom she remembered constantly. And she would say to herself, smiling at the blond fantasy: "If I must get married when I'm older, I would like to marry Bela."

Several years passed—oh, how slowly for the impatient Sarolta! Bela must have reached the age of twenty, and Terka, seventeen. They were still on the Riviera. And Sarolta grieved through the joyless, long years, which were lit up only by the illusion of a dream.

One violet evening, she was dreaming by her window when her mother came to tell her that Bela had returned. . . .

Sarolta's heart sang as if it would break. And, the next day, Bela same to see her.

He was the same, and even more charming than before. Sarolta was happy that he had kept this feminine and gentle manner which had so pleased her. He was still the fragile child. . . . But now this child possessed an inexpressible grace. Sarolta searched in vain for the cause of this transformation which made him so alluring. His voice was musical and faraway like the echo of the mountains. She admired everything about him, even his stone-grey English suit. And she even admired his mauve necktie.

Bela contemplated the young woman with different eyes, with eyes strangely beautiful, with eyes that did not resemble the eyes of other men. . . .

"How thin he is!" observed Sarolta's mother after he had left. "Poor thing, he must still be in delicate health."

Sarolta did not answer. She closed her eyes in order to again see Bela under her closed eyelids. . . . How handsome, handsome, handsome, he was! . . .

He returned the next day, and every day after that. He was the Prince Charming who is seen only in the childish pages of fairy tales. She could not look him in the face without feeling ardently and languishingly faint. . . . Her face changed according to the expression of the face she loved. Her heart beat according to the rhythm of that other heart. Her unconscious and childish tenderness had become love.

Bela would turn pale as soon as she appeared diaphanous in her white summer dress. Sometimes he looked at her without speaking, like someone communing with himself in front of a faultless statue. Sometimes he took her hand. . . . His palm was so burning and dry that she thought she was touching the hand of an invalid. Indeed, at those times a little fever would show in Bela's cheeks.

One day she asked him for some news of the undisciplined Terka.

"She is still in Nice," he answered indifferently. And then they spoke of something else. Sarolta understood that Bela did not love his sister at all. This was not surprising, what is more — a girl who was so taciturn and wild!

What should come next, came next. A few months later Bela asked to marry her. He had just turned twenty-one. Sarolta's mother had no objections to the union.

Their betrothal was unreal, as delicate as the white roses that Bela brought each day. Their vows were more fervent than poems; their very souls trembled on their lips. The nuptial dream came to be in the deepest silence.

"Why," Sarolta would ask her fiancé, "are you worthier of being loved than other young men? Why do you have gentle ways that they do not? Where did you learn the divine words that they never say?"

The wedding ceremony took place in absolute privacy. The candles brightened the red highlights in Bela's blond hair. The incense curled towards him, and the thunder of the organs exalted and glorified him. For the first time since the beginning of the world, the Groom was as beautiful as the Bride.

They left for those blue shores where the desire of lovers runs out of patience. They were seen, a Divine Couple, with the eyelashes of one stroking the eyelids of the other. They were seen, lovingly and chastely intertwined, with her black hair spread over his blond hair. . . .

Oh, my curious, little girl! Here the story becomes a little difficult to relate . . . Several months later, the real Bela Szecheny appeared. . . . He was not Prince Charming, alas! He was only a handsome boy, nothing more.

He furiously sought the identity of the young usurper. . . . And he learned that the usurper in question was his own sister, Terka.

. . . Sarolta and Prince Charming have never returned to Hungary. They are hiding in the depths of a Venetian castle or of a Florentine mansion. And sometimes they are seen, as one sees a vision of ideal tenderness, lovingly and chastely intertwined.

JANICE DABNEY

HATTIE

Old Hattie said she had chewed tobacco all her life. "But all the women still like to kiss me," she'd tease. Most of the time now her eyes were covered with thick tinted glasses — her only concession to failing sight while she pursued her favorite pastime. The way she strutted across the playing field, one never would have guessed she was almost blind. The slight hunch and the spit-and-polish orthopedic shoes ("My damn ankles gave out on me ten years back") only added to her stature: the Queen Mother of the Green, having played longer than all others on the Palo Alto Lawn Bowling Team.

No one else seemed to have the grace Hattie had developed, the intimate gestures she made, her studied waiting until it was her turn to place the weighted "bowl" and then her body dance, the slight lean to the left while aiming. She could not stand anything but pure silence as she aimed, and when the ball was freed to follow course, the air held that moment of after-prayer, her arm still extended as the black form approached the white. When she stood on the sidelines examining opponents' moves, she became a woman who had waited for trains all her life: shifting the bit of tobacco to the other cheek, forever watching with an air of expectation.

She never talked about her marriage except to say that it had ended years ago. But fragments of conversation — "I could never pin myself down to one place," "Just keeping your money without spending it is bad for the bowels," "When I am about to play a tournament, I need to be completely alone" — let one know the independent spirit had always been there.

Before her eyesight faded, she had painted to release the inner need for expression that had always kept her active. Now this energy found its way through talking, her fingers and arms moving constantly, or by concentrating long hours on Bach. In groups, she might relate the history of lawn bowling ("The second oldest sport, next to archery"). She might describe the mathematical precision of rolling an uneven object along a close-cut surface.

At night with only her cat Maxine, she would lean back in her chair, shift a slight bit to the left, and marvel at the Baroque equations being placed in air, giving her fresh sight. "Bach and bowling are what this life is all about," she would muse time and again, breathing lightly on her thick glasses to clear them before the next round.

CAROLINE OVERMAN

THE BACK RUB

The farm. Tuesday. 10:15 a.m. Our visitor arrives! I don't know what I'd expected, but find myself retreating to my notebook and recording details with great care, the way I do when something large is happening and I need time to understand it.

She is about my age and height, with glasses and short hair, but softly feminine in all the places I'm butch. Graceful as a dancer she moves easily with the flow of conversation, slight whiffs of perfume drifting to me now and then when her feelings are intense. I begin to experience a sort of aching attraction to her, a deep longing to stroke that dark curly hair, kiss the tender brow, and the soft curve of neck above her collar. Waves of heat engulf me. The conversation takes on a level of sexual innuendo, and I hear myself laughing and talking a little too loudly.

Eventually, the others go out to work and we are left alone. I grope for something to say, but she seems distracted, and finally confesses her back is aching. My mind races. I could offer to rub it. But do I dare? And can I confine myself to what is medically appropriate? I want to touch her so badly I stop caring if I make a fool of myself.

"Would you like me to give you a back rub?" I ask.

"That would be wonderful," she answers. Either she hasn't noticed the tremor in my voice or she has decided to ignore it.

Turning her back modestly she removes her shirt, then unfastens her jeans and lies down on the bed. I am relieved she hasn't taken them off too. The shirt is already more than I had bargained for. To cover my confusion, I begin reading aloud the label on the bottle of massage oil. It isn't mine but this is no time for social niceties. I pour out a reckless amount and straddle her, forcing myself not to look at how her thighs push taut against the jeans, and her backbone disappears into the crack of her ass.

Slowly. carefully, I slide my fingers up her back, around the bunched neck muscles and out along her shoulders. "Mmm, that feels good." Encouraged, I work my way down again. This time the neck muscles aren't so tight, and I begin to have a clearer sense of her body. I grip her thighs between my knees and let myself rock forward, leaning my weight more firmly down my arms and onto her back. Her skin, slippery now from the oil, offers no resistance as my thumbs circle and smooth the knots along her spine. Up and down, around and down, up and around and down, down.

I grow bolder; I stop moving and just hold my hands on her, pouring my heat into her. She lies still and relaxed, breathing into my hands. I try to slow my breath to match hers, then forget to breathe at all as I draw my fingers lightly down her sides, just grazing the swelling breasts. She sighs and seems to settle her body more closely against me. I lift her shoulders gently, and feel her opening to me, trusting me to hold her. My touch is now more a caress than a massage as I slide my fingers down her arms to her wrists, her palms, until my fingers curl in hers and she is squeezing them back. Did I imagine that? No, she squeezes them again, and I am making love to both her hands and she is letting me. The need to clasp her against me is so overwhelming I stop thinking of the consequences and simply lie down on top of her, kissing her neck, her cheek, and anything else I can reach. "Oh God that feels good," I breathe. "Yes," she answers, "oh yes."

We became lovers more fully that night, then spent the year with other women, on opposite sides of the country, and didn't write. When I saw her again a year later, I knew I still wanted her. I pursued her for a week without success. Ironically, before she flew back to her other lover, she told our friends, "Caroline offered to give me a back rub when I had my period, but I turned her down. I know where that leads!"

CANYON SAM

LEAF PEEKING IN VERMONT*

Greyhound from New York City to White River Junction, transfer White River Junction to Vermont Transit. For this first leg of my journey, I take a window seat in the third row on the right-hand side of the bus. People are piling on — knocking their baggage and belongings up the narrow aisle as they search for a seat.

"Is this seat taken?" asks a small woman in a black coat. Diminutive, with blinking eyes and fussy mannerisms, she is in her late sixties. "I don't want to sit in the back because of the smoke," she says angrily.

"Don't mind me, I'm grumpy this morning," she says, settling into her seat, her face tense as she darts glances at the seats around her checking their occupants.

"I'm grumpy sometimes too," I laugh. Though not today. I'm in a good mood today: relaxed and excited having just spent two fabulous weeks in New York City. I start up a friendly chat as she seems very nervous.

She's going to Hanover to visit her niece; I'm going to Montpelier to visit a friend of a friend on a sheep farm. I ask if she knows the route the bus will be taking so I can follow along on my map of Connecticut and Massachusetts. It turns out she lives just blocks from where I stayed in New York, on East 88th and 1st Avenue. After a while, she has told me about her life — how she wakes at 5:30 and bathes; waters her plants; waits at the doorstep of the supermarket at 8 when it opens so she can do her shopping; stands in line outside the bank when it opens at 9; and stays in in the afternoon reading books and sewing.

She tells me she has a Japanese hairdresser, who is very nice,

---

*This is an excerpt from a longer work, four stories titled *New England Suite.*

and that she likes miso soup, which she thinks is very good.

In no time she's more at ease. Now I find the problem is getting her to stop talking to me. I want to stare at all the passing foliage, the constantly changing view of hills and woodlands and birch forests all rust, orange, glittering golden.

She seems intent now on being my tour guide.

"You see now dear, these are the maple trees. You see? You see there?" She grabs my arm with her tiny white-gloved hand. "You see the shape of the leaf? Yes, those are maples."

I pick up my novel and submerge myself in the pages, because when I look out the window she thinks it's because I have nothing to do, and nothing's being said, so she talks to my turned shoulder.

She has taken me under her wing thinking, I'm sure, that because I am young and so far from home, traveling alone to a part of the country I've never been before, surely I would welcome friendly local guidance. I don't mind hospitality, but when she offers it, she speaks to me as if to a child.

The bus stops briefly in a small town in Connecticut, and I say I am going to the bathroom. She takes my arm in her little vise grip and shows me exactly where the restroom is, even though finding a restroom in a Greyhound station is about as difficult as finding fast food in a McDonald's.

Shortly after the driver announces that we're going through Danbury, Connecticut, home of the Duracell battery, she decides that we are getting along so well that now we can speak of more personal matters:

"I hope you don't mind my saying this, but I was reading this book on race . . . and you know what I learned that I hadn't known before? That you Oriental people don't have sweat glands under your arms! Isn't that something? I didn't know that! I read that and I went down to my hairdresser—like I told you she's Japanese—and I said: 'Is it true that Orientals don't have sweat glands under their arms?' And she said it was!"

I tell her that it's not true; as a matter of fact, it's preposterous. Of course, Asian people have sweat glands under their arms.

She answers just as incredulously: "Really, really? You do? You do have sweat glands under your arms? Well . . . I would write that author a letter and tell him he's wrong, but he's dead (the book is called *Race*, written by a man named James Baker in 1947).

After we've settled that one she continues: "I also read in that book that Aryans don't like crowded conditions. Yes, I notice that. I don't like crowds. When I have to shop downtown, I am waiting right at Gimbels' doorstep at 10 o'clock when they open; I do my business and I'm out by 11, because everyone else starts coming after that."

I have a very clear picture of the dinner table at Beth's house the night before I left after having Rosh Hashana with Beth and her friends. I ask what New England is like and Amanda describes the land, the autumn, the people, but what she ends with is: "But I don't know what it'd be like for a Third World person there." It's not taking me a hell of a long time to find out.

The next morning, Elly and I drive the few miles into Jefferson-ville to have breakfast at a local inn. The breathtakingly gorgeous countryside is rich in fall colors. On the way, Elly points out the local high school with pride; just completed last year, it is a spacious, modern complex which takes in all the students who used to go to four different small high schools. It's on lovely rolling pasture land, and when the football team practices they have to chase the cows off the football field. When they finish using it, the cows wander back and graze.

When we get to town I step out of the car in front of the inn: the white icicle steeple of a church across the street surrounded by majestic red and yellow birch trees sparkles under a piercing blue sky in the cold morning sunlight.

It's like a picture postcard: turn it over and it would say "photograph of the heart of America."

California was California. But California as we knew it was never what we learned of in American literature or read about in history class. The pictures in textbooks were never of Malibu

beach or the Mojave Desert of even Yosemite Valley—they
were of scenes like this: the old New England church in autumn
. . . its clean white steeple in the crisp clear air. *This* earth knows
America's earliest beginnings in its deepest soil. *This* was really
America, its root and its heart. California has never been more
than a wayward child.

We have eggs and sausages in the inn, the walls of which are
warmly decorated with watercolors by local artists and pictures
of whaling ships, the windows adorned with bright, billowing
curtains. It's charming and friendly and down to earth. We share
a relaxed breakfast with soft pop music playing over the inn's
stereo. The news comes over the air shortly after we start eating:
there was a book burning last night at a church in Burlington, a
town twenty minutes away. Crowds burned Hemingway's *The
Sun Also Rises*, Elvis Presley records, James Brown tapes.

The next day's paper goes into more depth: Rock music prompts
sex, drugs, rebellion. It's the music of the devil and the goat's
head is its symbol. This music has induced sexual orgasms in
young girls who stood in front of speakers playing it at rock
concerts. Records have been tested and discovered to contain
the chant "Smoke Marijuana" when played backwards. It was a
frenzied scene in Burlington with the 29-year-old priest exhorting,
admonishing, and finally leading his listeners outside to the
church parking lot where people threw books into a flaming bon-
fire, teenagers tossed record albums, the crowd gripped hands
and prayed. Women sobbed. Men shouted curses at the devil and
shook their fists into the night air. People cried out Glory Alleluia
at each toss of a record album, paperback collection, or old dog-
eared novel into the leaping, crackling flames. Glory Alleluia.

Two local goat farmers then admitted to the newspaper that in
the past year they have found goats beheaded in a ritualistic
manner.

This is America now. Not San Francisco. My island, San Francisco. This is America. And it's absolutely sobering.

JANE RULE

LESBIAN AND WRITER:
MAKING THE REAL VISIBLE

I am a politically involved lesbian, and I am a writer. I do not see the two as mutually exclusive; neither do I see them as inextricably bound together. Yet one of those two conflicting views is held by most people who read my work. The editors of *Chatelaine*, for instance, would as soon their readers weren't reminded that the writer of the Harry and Anna stories, affectionately and humorously concerned with family life, is also the author of *Lesbian Images*. Most critics of my novels, on the other hand, use my sexuality to measure all my characters. Those who are lesbian are naturally the most persuasive. My male characters are considered weak. Even for those not so crudely tempted, I am judged as remarkably fair to all my characters when one considers that I am, after all, a lesbian. For critics who are themselves gay, I am held politically accountable for every less-than-perfect gay character and I am warned that I will lose a large part of my audience if I insist on including heterosexual characters in my work. And in the academy, I am dismissed as a marginal writer not because some of my characters share my sexuality but because I am a lesbian, therefore somehow mysteriously disqualified from presenting a vision of central value.

Kind, straight friends have argued that, if I weren't so visibly a lesbian, my work wouldn't be so often distorted and dismissed. But short of denying my sexuality, there is little I can do. It is not I but the interviewer or reviewer who is more interested in the fact that I am a lesbian than in the fact that I am a writer. My only positive choice under the circumstance is to use the media to make educational points about my sexuality.

Many people in the gay movement do not understand why I don't use my work as I am often willing to use myself for propaganda. Though one heterosexual critic did call *Lesbian Images* a piece of propaganda because in it I make my own bias quite clear, even that book does not satisfy the homosexual propagandists who would have me not waste time on politically incorrect lesbian writers like Radclyffe Hall, May Sarton, Maureen Duffy—in fact, nearly all the writers I studied in depth, but concentrate only on my most radical contemporaries, who are writing experimental erotica and separatist utopias.

I decided to be a writer not because I was a great reader as a child or had any natural gift for language but because I wanted to speak the truth as I saw it. To understand and share that understanding has been my preoccupation since I was in my teens. No political or moral ideal can supercede my commitment to portray people as they really are. What is is my domain. What ought to be is the business of politicians and preachers.

It is still a popular heterosexual belief that all homosexuals are at least sick and probably depraved, and they should, therefore, be, if not incarcerated in mental hospitals and jails, at least invisible. It is the conviction of many gay militants that all homosexuals are victims and martyrs who must become heroically visible so that everyone will have to face the fact that education, industry, the law, medicine, and the government would all come to a grinding halt without the homosexuals who are the backbone of all our institutions. "Even Eleanor Roosevelt . . ." that argument can begin or end. The truth of experience lies elsewhere.

For offering a balanced view of society, I'm sure I know a disproportionate number of homosexuals, as I know a disproportionate number of artists, white people, Canadians. One of the truths about all of us is that we live in disproportionate groups. That is why novels tend to be full of Jews or Blacks or soldiers or Englishmen or heterosexuals. Very few tend to be full of homosexuals because, until recently, homosexuals didn't live in social groups except in some places in Europe. My first two novels, *Desert of the Heart* and *This Is Not For You*, though they are about lesbian relationships, are not full of lesbians. I was writing about what was ardent, dangerous and secret, which is what lesbian experience still is for a great number of people. In my third novel, *Against the Season*, which was the beginning of my preoccupation with groups of people rather than with one or two main characters, out of about a dozen characters two are lesbian. There are a gay male and a lesbian in my fourth novel, *The Young in One Another's Arms*, out of a cast of about ten. Three and a half of eight characters are homosexual in my latest novel, *Contract with the World*. In all of my novels my gay characters move in an essentially heterosexual world as most gay people do. Though some of them are closeted in that world, some punished and defeated by it, they are all visible to the reader who is confronted with who they are and how they feel.

In a rare and beautiful comment about a character in *Contract with the World*, Leo Simpson says, "When Allen is arrested on some kind of homosexual charge, he has become so real that the laws of society immediately seem barbarous. Comfortable prejudices look like a tyranny of fear, which is of course part of what Rule's novel wants to say."

Yes, exactly, not heroic or saintly but *real*, and it is *part* of what I want to say. But in this book I am basically concerned with six or eight people, each of whom deals with barbarous law and comfortable prejudice, not always to do with homosexuality or even sexuality. What gathers the characters into one book is their involvement with art in a provincial city far from any cultural centre. To be an artist in this country is very difficult. To deal with the pain and doubt and wonder of such aspirations is my chief preoccupation in this book. My characters are neither necessarily greatly talented nor superior in vision simply because they are artists. They all have to face the fact that, except for the few greatest, artists are considered failures. A great many, very gifted or not, can't stand such a climate. In this they share something of the strain it is to be homosexual in a homophobic culture.

I owe to my own art all the honesty and insight I have, not simply about homosexuals and artists, both of which I happen to be, but about the whole range of my experience as a member of a family, a community, a country. I don't write Harry and Anna stories to cater to *Chatelaine*'s heterosexual readers though I like the cheques well enough when they come in. (No one could eat writing for *Christopher Street*, and I still give most of my short fiction away.) I write them out of affection for those men and women, like my own parents, who care for and love and enjoy their children and because I, too, have cared for and loved and enjoyed children. There are heterosexual men and women in all my work because there are heterosexual men and women in my life and world, to whom I owe much of my understanding.

A blind writer once said to me, "You're the only writer I know who includes characters who happen to be physically handicapped. In most fiction, if they are there at all, it's *because* they're handicapped." That for me is the real distinction between what I write and propaganda. I am trying to make the real visible. People "happen to be" a lot of things about which there are cultural phobias. I have never found either safety or comfort in a blind heart, as a way to work or live.

As a lesbian, I believe it is important to stand up and be counted, to insist on the dignity and joy loving another woman is for me. If that gets in the way of people's reading my books, I have finally to see that it is their problem and not mine. As a writer, I must be free to say what is in all the diversity I can command. I regret the distorting prejudices that surround me, whether they affect homosexuals or men or the physically handicapped, and I can't alone defeat them. They will not defeat me, either as a lesbian or a writer.

SDIANE BOGUS

TO MY MOTHER'S VISION

The writing of this essay is evidence, again, of my insistent impulse to write, and more. It symbolizes yet another attempt to crystallize my dream of being somebody, of acknowledging the life of my mother, of solidifying my wish for literary greatness. As I look back over the last ten years, those that represent my professional career, I see how far I've come, and I sigh to think that I may still have very far to go.

What have been my steps along the writing path, you may ask? They have been slow, mincing, and occasionally encouraged by others who I have passed along the way. The impulse to write itself sprang full-blown inside me when I was nine or ten. It throbbed into existence as a result of my two brothers having had a poem and an editorial, respectively, published in our elementary school newspaper. Envy, pride, and awe unfettered within me some latent urge to write; and ever since, I have wanted to be the somebody that the admiring school populace recognized. To my knowledge, they never wrote anything else publishable or creative, but from that happenstance in 1955, I became insatiably "turned on" to the printed word and was intent on plummeting the depths of my self and soul to produce words that, once printed, would blind my reader with envy, awe, and pride.

My earliest reader was my mother; a lover of poetry herself, she often quoted Longfellow from memory as she went about the harsh chores of our cold-water flat. I'd come dashing home from school in those latter days following the publication of the "Bogus boys," and plop my new "hearts and flowers" creation before her. With the eloquence of Sojourner Truth, she'd intake a breath, and read aloud the sentimental, slightly unrhythmical, "mistress-piece" (apologies to traditionalists). On one of those days, she declared, "You're going to be a writer when you grow up. I think I'll get you a typewriter when you become sixteen."

What age was I then? Eleven? Twelve? Thirteen? I don't know; it doesn't matter because I've never forgotten the moment. What she had done was to define me, to offer the future to me, to approve of my talent, to encourage it. That day, I stood before her as she sat in bed; she was ill. My heart pounded anticipatorily as if age sixteen was a moment or two away. I stood there dreaming of legions of readers, legions who would, like my mother, read my work, not with envy, but love, pride and awe. Her declaration of my future had slain envy of my brothers and other writers, and I was free to become a writer compared to none. Oh, how I dreamed!

Waiting for sixteen, I churned out poems and stories with the facility of a first-grade finger-painter. I marveled at my ability; and to get better at it, I would read books during my school's "library hour" in order to get an idea of how I'd want my books to be when I grew up. I read The White Stag, Caddie Woodlawn, Alexander Hamilton the Young Lion, and many others. Outside of school, I visited the public library like a nun goes to prayer, habitually, religiously, and seriously.

By now, my mother was in the hospital in Chicago, and I was living with an aunt on the other side of town. Children under sixteen weren't allowed to visit people in the hospital, so I mailed my staple-bound notebooks to my mother. She wrote back, infrequently, commending my vocabulary, my ideas, and reminding me of the promised typewriter come my sixteenth year. I was fourteen then, but my anticipation remained great. My dreams were grand. My writing advanced (for a ninth grader). My mother died. She died young, died of cancer, died of overwork and worry and Blackness in an underpaid, poor person's factory job.

No single setback to my career has ever been as devastating as that first one. With my mother dead so were my dreams. She had been the repository for them. She would have been the one to make them real and official by buying me a typewriter. But she was dead and so was the writer in me. I did not write again for two years.

Meanwhile I was shipped from Chicago to Birmingham, Alabama, because my father did not think he could raise me without my mother. I was enrolled in high school, and I promptly fell in love with one of my schoolmates, the girl next door. It was a hide and seek affair. We hid to kiss and fondle, and sought a means to do it again and again. She reminded me of my mother, and some time around 1962, I wrote a poem that exorcised my grief and resurrected my talent:

TO MY MOTHER

Though Death took you from me
While yet in younger years
I feel, Dear Mother, in time of need,
Your memory calms my fears.
I wondered on the day, they laid you away,
My eyes full of tears and sorrow
Oh, Mother, I loved you so
What's in store for tomorrow?

Although not printed in its entirety, the poem represents my having come to terms with my mother's death, but the question remained, what did life have to offer?

Well, upon my second Christmas with my grandmother, aunt, and uncle, I was given a typewriter! Miraculously, it came a month shy of my sixteenth birthday. Up to that point my relatives had seen me scrawl out several of my notebook paper books, and I guess my creative insistence convinced them that I was serious. Surely, a typewriter could help me with my schoolwork.

By graduation from high school, I had written eight to ten of those stapled paper books, as well as kept tedious diaries. I had not yet been discovered to be *gay* (though my family was suspicious of my odd intimacy with my girlfriend—we just *had* to be together many hours beyond school) and I had read enough of Edgar Allan Poe to be able to call him "an influence of mine." I only regret one thing about those racially segregated days of the

South of the early sixties, that I did not have a teacher in a position to get my work in *The Birmingham News* as did the teachers of the white kids. On any given day, Johnny White Boy or Mary White Girl grinned from the front page or the editorial page as his or her poem or essay ran an impressive column or two to their creative credit, and that credit always went indirectly to the person who'd discovered or submitted Johnny's or Mary's work, most often a teacher. It wasn't easy to be a Black student and receive that kind of recognition, because it wasn't easy to be a Black teacher and recommend it.

It wasn't that I did not take my work to school and show it around; I did, to this student editor of the newspaper or to that teacher or counselor, but none of them said, "Let me see if I can get this published." None of them put me onto newspapers or magazines where I might submit myself. The most I got was "This is good." "You write well." "Keep on writing." Not that I was unencouraged by their responses, but I didn't want to keep my little stapled books of poems in a drawer at home. I had dreams. I had hopes. There were legions of readers waiting to be blinded by the brilliance of my words, weren't there?

Nineteen-sixty-four took me to Stillman College, where, while I pursued my B.A. in English, I began a literary magazine, and came in conflict with my sexual preference. This struggle is detailed in an autobiographical short story called "A Measure by June." So, suffice it to say, that at Stillman I was known as a talented writer but also as a "bull dagger," and I didn't know if that combination would get me very far in life. I had a girlfriend and there was a lot of talk about us. But my being a writer played into my winning a fellowship to Syracuse University. My impulse to write was now fired by a hope that I could go on to become a great writer despite my color and sexual preference. The way to do it was to avoid writing especially Black stories, and to hide my being homosexual. The deterrent of being a woman writer hadn't occurred to me yet, but I was suspicious about why it was that only men writers seem to be celebrated in America.

Before trucking off to Syracuse in 1968 to undertake my M.A.

studies, I submitted a batch of poems to Nikki Giovanni. She accepted one of my poems for her first anthology, *Night Comes Softly*. Although my plan was to avoid writing on Black themes, I had already done so. The transition and rhetoric of the middle 60s created a "Black consciousness" for me, and on reading much Baldwin, Hughes, and Wright—on my own, as an undergraduate— I wrote endless poems about Black and racial matters.

Once at Syracuse, I had no luck publishing in the university magazine, but unable to resist the fury that reading *The Autobiography of Malcolm X* inspired in me, I created more "Black" poems. None of them were published, though I could now boast of one prospective market, *Negro Digest*. By the time I left Syracuse, I not only had reams of unpublished poetry, but short stories in great numbers. If nothing else, my craft was undergoing a prolonged developmental period.

I had no lover in Syracuse, and that was probably for the best. I was not at all settled about being gay. The fact was, I was still a bit surprised by it. I had been groomed to be a petite and neat heterosexual, and for many years, I'd played out my socialization. In Syracuse I dated men, hiding my preference from them and myself. Once graduated, though, in 1969, I was hired by Miles College. Still unpublished, I returned to Birmingham to teach freshman studies, hoping against evidence that things would change.

At Miles things did change; my work began to be accepted regularly by the college newspaper, *Black Flame*. People began to ask if I planned a book of poems or if I had tried to publish a book. From these people I learned where to submit. Gathering my poems together that reflected the same theme, I began circulating what would become *I'm Off to See the Goddamn Wizard, Alright!* Meanwhile, I allowed myself to fall in love with a female student.

A young lesbian myself, never really having had an opportunity to live with a woman or know the responsibility and maturity that takes, I soon let the entire campus become aware of the "affair," and before long, I was asked not to come back the next year. That was a blow. In Birmingham, news affecting the Black community travels like lightning down a metal rod. I was soon the town's gossip plate and the shame of my family. So, I packed up my little red VW, and trucked off to Chicago where my two brothers and my father were still living. My student-lover managed to get her brother to bring her to Chicago.

By the fall of 1970, Giovanni's book had come out, and seeing "Dippity Did/Done" in print made me want to have that proud experience again, and again. Now, in the midst of teaching tenth-grade English for the Chicago Board of Education and setting up housekeeping with my student-lover, I wrote Nikki to acknowledge the publication and ask for leads to publishers. She wrote back suggesting Broadside Press and Third World Press; both were near by. She also mentioned that Gwendolyn Brooks lived in Chicago, as well as Don L. Lee, a radical new Black poet who was getting much exposure from the chapbooks that he had self-published in rapid succession.

I contacted the lot of them. Lee and Brooks didn't answer at first. Broadside rejected the *Wizard* manuscript outright. I was crushed, but not beaten. I believed in my work. I didn't know why, but I did. My mother had said I could write. Who could dispute the perspicuity of a mother? Besides, it was utterly important to me to make her vision and hope for me come true now. I didn't want her life to have been pointless. I would be somebody. I would be great. I may be homosexual, I told myself, but that won't stand in the way of my art. If I'm good, I'm just good. Look at Baldwin. Look at Langston Hughes. Look at Gwen Brooks!

Gwen Brooks. That was it! One wintery Saturday morning, frustrated by having received innumerable rejection notices from Grove Press, Third World, Johnson Publications, and hordes more, I dressed warmly and drove, manuscript in tow, to her house. Afraid that she might not be there, afraid that she'd think I was crazy to just come to her house unannounced, I took a frosty deep breath and marched brazenly up the stairs of that dismally grey abode on Evans Street. I rang the bell. No answer. I rang it again. No answer. I looked at my watch. Oh, God! It was seven-thirty a.m. I hadn't realized how early it was. Now I panicked. Oh,

God what a bad impression of me she'd have if she opened the door now. And who the hell would want to see any damn poetry at seven-thirty in the morning? I decided to leave quickly, but before I could get off the porch, I heard a voice mew, "Who is it?"

"Diane Bogus," I confessed weakly. At that time, I hadn't taken on the authorial SDiane persona.

To my surprise, she invited me in, the kind soul, and I waited while she dressed. She informed me in a muffled voice from another room in the house that she was just about to get ready to take a bus to a place on 63rd Street, and from there she would be going down to the Loop. She said she didn't have much time because Saturdays were very busy for her. I apologized for barging in on her, but I did not say I would leave. I just had to know her opinion of my work, and I said so. I offered to drive her wherever she had to go if she would just look over my poems as we rode. She agreed.

In the car, she read several of my poems aloud. I marveled at her interpretations. She got their tones and rhythms. She enunciated their softnesses and angers. She projected my messages. I paid attention. Although I had a strong poetic voice, I felt my natural one could not dramatize the deep feelings that characterized my work. Emitting several approving "Hmmmms," and an occasional, "I like this one," she invited me to come back to her house the next day. She said Dudley Randall of Broadside Press would be there, and she'd share my work with him. I didn't tell her he had already rejected it. Maybe with her "pull" she might change his mind.

Except for the point where she showed me how to read my work, the visit was a failure. Randall read my work, some of it aloud. I remember the stricken distasteful expression that crossed his face when he realized that "Black Ecstasy" was a lesbian love poem. No doubt, this was what had displeased him and many of my potential publishers. That poem wasn't the only one of its kind in the book. Soon Randall was theorizing about poetics, and challenging some of the ideas within my work. Hearing his censure, Brooks was closemouthed where she had been supportive the

the day before. We kicked around ideas about the poems of Sonia Sanchez, Don L. Lee, Hoyt Fuller, and Nikki Giovanni. All of them, along with Brooks and Randall, appeared regularly in *Negro Digest*. I applauded this work, except for Fuller's. But what put them off the most was a poem I had written about Angela Davis, entitled, "Remember What Happened to King Kong?" It opened, "If I were Angela, I would kill myself." I felt that Angela was being exploited commercially, and I advocated suicide to end the misapplication of her dedication to Black liberation. We debated the issue round. They wouldn't take me seriously. They said, "You can't mean that." They were quietly appalled. The air became stale and unaccepting. Brooks asked me to read one of my poems to break the impasse. I hurriedly chattered a Christmas poem called, "A Dream like Daniel's," to which she cried. "No, no, that's not the way that poem is to be read!" Then, taking the page from my hands, *she* read it, as well as my mother would have, as well as Sojourner would have. Then she made me read it again. My reading pleased her. "That's better," she said. I was pleased, too. I went away, no publisher gained, and no acceptance earned into their closed circle of writers, but I did learn how to read my work.

Some time later, unannounced, Don L. Lee showed up at my apartment. I was surprised. He came with my manuscript in hand. He wanted to advise me. He cut me down. He said I was trite and imitative. He said I had some good poems in the book, but he wouldn't tell me which. He wanted me to struggle to get better. That way I could exceed even my best. I was deflated. I needed to know what I had done right so I could do some more of it. He was aggressively against positive criticism. After serving his dutiful poetic function, he cunningly asked me to go out with him. I found that tactless and ruinous of my image of literary decorum. I asked him out of my apartment. Spitefully, in a matter of months, I had saved enough money from my teaching salary to publish the book myself.

Four hundred copies and no distributor later, at the end of December, 1971, my brothers, friends and I had sold over half of the copies. The rest were gone by May. I do remember two specific incidents that broke my heart, though. Ambitious, sure of the worth of that offset, odd-sized paper cover book of poems, I sent it off to Johnny Carson. I had the nerve to want to be interviewed on "The Tonight Show." NBC sent me a courteous rejection and their best wishes.

At another point, Aretha Franklin was in town, and I managed to get backstage to give her an autographed copy of the book, and was allowed to hang out in her dressing room to chat for as long as I pleased. Feeling the chasm between my art and hers, I signed the book, asking for her feedback, took her autograph on a program, and left. A week later, someone rang my doorbell, and when I called down through the intercom to inquire who it was, someone answered "Aretha." I nearly croaked from the honor. I bolted to the door only to find some stranger coming up the stairs, who discovered, as I did, that she had pushed the wrong bell.

The struggles and problems associated wi th the publication of *I'm Off to See the Goddamn Wizarad, Alright!* didn't go unrecognized, though. Somehow one of the review copies that I had sent out reached the hands of a Chicago librarian, Alfred Woods, who knew Tony Phillips, the PBS moderator of the Black talk show, "Harambee." Woods liked my work so much he secured me an interview on that show. Luckily, I had learned to read my work aloud. Success was on its way!

This story goes on through my relationship with my student-lover, who interfered with my writing to the point where we broke up. There was constant friction because on the weekends, when I wanted to write, she wanted attention. We had other domestic problems, too, and I left for California. By that time, in 1973, my work had more of a feminist accent, through my contact with "women-identified-women"—lesbians. Out of these associations *Woman in the Moon* was created. A woman in the East agreed to publish both this book and *Wizard*, but she put illustrations she hadn't cleared with me in *Woman in the Moon* and the book was really tacky looking. She never finished the second book. I lost $1400. Then a woman in California with a new publicity agency said she'd get *Woman in the Moon* back in print, but suddenly she decided to go to Washington, D.C., and she left me with only the paste-up boards. I'd given her $1500. So I was ripped off twice by women publishers. This was heartbreaking, but I still held onto the faith that my work was destined to see the light. I raised the money a third time and managed to publish *Woman in the Moon* myself.

By now I have long since come to terms with my lesbianism, its effects on my career, as well as the effect of my Blackness and womanness on it. I never really dealt with them as issues, but kept my eyes on the stars. Greatness rests not in the hands of those who don't perceive it, nor can it be a dream deferred by racial, sexual or biological prejudice. Through the support of friends and family, sometimes even colleagues, I have always raised money to publish my books. I suspect, as long as I am unpublished by others, I'll be a do-it-yourselfer.

Although I've had a number of successes that cut across the writing genres, my family members, other than my brothers, don't quite realize that I am known as a writer. Although I send home newsclippings and photos from reading performances, I think they still view me as a wild, foolish woman who will eventually be sorry that she did not marry, have a family and rely on a man for support. To them I will probably grow old alone. To them, my writing is some extended childhood fantasy, and it's a good thing that I went to school and "got my education" because this "writing stuff" hasn't ever paid off.

But it has paid off enough to keep me at it. One of my lovers bought me my first subscriptions to *Writer's Digest* and *The Writer*. Another gave me the earnings on her life insurance to defray the cost of publishing *Woman in the Moon* after I had been burned.

Meanwhile, the diversity of my writing has prevented the wide knowledge of my work. I published science fiction in *Diversifier* and *Space and Time*, for example, and articles in mainstream home and family magazines, *Valley View* of Ohio to name one. My reviews appeared in *Black Scholar* and *Black Thought*, and my gay stories in *Azalea, Lesbian Tide* and other small press publications. Since my audience has been scattered, it has been difficult for readers to follow my career. Yet with the publication of JR Roberts' *Black Lesbians*, more people are interested in what I've been writing and what I think. I am happy for this new measure of success, but it does not yet appear that I am home free. I am struggling now to raise money for the publication of an anthology of my latest poems, short stories and essays.

Early in my writing career, I wanted to be read with love, awe, and pride. Now I want to be read for my vision, for my wisdom, for my truths. I'd like to leave a legacy of uniqueness akin to Gertrude Stein's, but I want it to be as full-bodied and meaningful as the life and writings of Martin Luther King, Jr.

This may or may not happen. Recently, a publisher for my novel, *Of Hallowed Things Talked Aloud*, withdrew from contract negotiations because we could not see eye to eye on God and race. Furthermore, I am still not being paid for my work. After ten years — this is the eleventh — one would think checks for publication would come more regularly than one or two every six or seven months. They don't; most often the work is featured gratis or for the price of a copy of the magazine it appears in. One would think that with all of the rabid commerce that the feminist and gay movement has inspired, there'd be money from those buttons, posters, cards, T-shirts, books, and the like to pay artists. There seems not to be.

Perhaps, when I am finally in a royalty receiving position, I can quit my mainline teaching, and be about my Mother's business in earnest, and that business is to be the finest writer I can be. I will need solitude for this, and maybe the Ph.D. that I am pursuing will allow me that space. I know somewhere inside me that even if I never see my work become as great as it in time will be acknowledged to be, I will keep on writing. I am aided by reading performances of my work. Cheryl Coleman, my musician lover, and I are currently exploring a mixed media presentation of our artistry.

This essay does not begin to scratch the surface of my growth as a writer nor accurately trace the paths over which I have come. There is no space to detail it all. Although I once swore I'd stop writing in ten years, if I had not attained the Pulitzer Prize, I didn't mean it. July 1983 marked the end of my ten year deadline and found me completing my dissertation, which just may win that prize.

Seeking to enhance myself as a writer by undertaking the study of American writers and the American writing traditions, I know of no better way to nourish my greatness than this intensive contact with the literary greats. In the end, I am sure this long incubation of my art will prove my mother correct—I will be a writer when I grow up.

PAM ANNAS

"AS COMMON AS THE BEST OF BREAD": JUDY GRAHN, PAT PARKER, AND WORKING CLASS POETRY

> I am the wall at the lip of the water
> I am the rock that refused to be battered
> I am the dyke in the matter, the other
> I am the wall with the womanly swagger
> Judy Grahn, She Who

> My lady is definitely no lady
> which is fine with me,
> cause i ain't no gentleman.
> Pat Parker, "My Lady Ain't No Lady"

Pat Parker and Judy Grahn are lesbian feminist poets, part of a radical tradition of women's poetry. They are also, as working class women, inheritors of a tradition of literature that has been denied and marginalized as the writing by women of any class. Pat Parker is black; Judy Grahn is white. They are both working class poets. Their claiming of their identity, their naming of themselves in their poetry, is based on a complex of factors of which gender is only one aspect. They are like other women poets/lesbian poets in their sense of being oppressed and misdefined by a patriarchal culture.[1] They are like other working class writers (men and women, white and black and immigrant) first in the sense of their uneasy relation to a class structure that excludes and misdefines them and, second, in the sense of not having the expectation of the economic privilege of a "class-ical" education and the implications that has for one's relation to and use of literary forms.

Working class literature has not been a high priority area in literary studies. Paul Lauter, Lawrence Levine, Dan Tannacito, and Martha Vicinus are among the few critics and historians of literature who have discussed the productions of working class

—112—

writers.[2] Tannacito categorizes the poetry which a group of Colorado miners published in their union magazine from 1903-1906 into six distinct types: work poems, poems of praise (of workers and working class heroes), poems of censure and condemnation (of the mine owners and their allies), poems of struggle, poems of solidarity, and aphorisms (which sum up and condense common experience). There are examples of all these types in the work of Pat Parker and Judy Grahn, though there are more poems about love than poems about work. Perhaps because love has been, historically, women's work. Or perhaps love is a predominant theme in the work of lesbian writers because who homosexuals love is both a definition (and a misdefinition) of self. I am struck by Grahn's and Parker's use of the aphorism which, in its brevity, its mnemonic quality, and its connection to an oral tradition, is a particularly working class and popular form. Pat Parker's "Brother" is aphoristic: "Brother/ I don't want to hear/ about/ how my real enemy/ is the system./ i'm no genius,/ but i do know/ that system/ you hit me with/ is called/ a fist." Many of the poems in Grahn's *Confrontations With the Devil in the Form of Love* are aphoristic.

> Love came along and saved me
> saved me   saved
> me.
> However, my life remains the same as before.
> O What shall I do now that I have
> what I've always been looking for?[3]

Although Pat Parker and Judy Grahn are self-consciously self-defined poets in a way that Tannacito's miners were not, their poetry shows the influence of their class origins and its particular "literary tradition."[4] As working class poetry, their poems tend to be narrative or sequential more often than lyrical. When they are not sequences (i.e., a series of connected poems that tell a story or make an argument), the poems tend to be either long or aphoristic and some of them—*Goat Child, Movement in Black,* and *Womanslaughter* by Pat Parker and *A Woman is Talking to*

Death by Judy Grahn—have an epic or dramatic quality. The poems are often argumentative and discursive as well as imagistic. Their purpose is to raise your consciousness, change your mind, move you to action as well as to laughter, tears, or serenity; they are explicitly political. The poems are oral, particularly Pat Parker's, which emerge from a black tradition of poetry that crosses class lines as well as from a working class tradition of poetry that crosses race lines.[5] The poems need to be heard. Like much working class poetry, these poems tend to be, in images, in concept, and in form, creatively derivative rather than necessarily original. Poets borrow lines and whole structures from each other and refine, particularize, or vary them in a way that is as close to folk tale and folk song as to "literature." For example, Pat Parker's *Womanslaughter* is based on Judy Grahn's *A Woman is Talking to Death. A Woman is Talking to Death* is based on earlier work by Pat Parker. Grahn's *Confrontations With the Devil in the Form of Love* is based on Ntozake Shange's *For Colored Girls Who Have Considered Suicide When the Rainbow is Enuf. For Colored Girls Who Have Considered Suicide When the Rainbow is Enuf* is in turn based on Grahn's *Common Woman Poems.* The poetry is shared in the making rather than owned; it is communal as well as individual.

The content of Pat Parker's and Judy Grahn's poems is the experience of being working class, as well as lesbian, woman, black or white. In *Goat Child*, Parker writes about her college years, when she felt she didn't own culture and ideas in the way people around her seemed to. This is an experience familiar to anyone from a working class background who finds herself in a middle class context. In an untitled poem, Parker identifies with the working class experience of her parents:

> My hands are big & rough
>   like my mother's
> my innards are twisted & torn
>   like my father's
> my self is

my big hands—
   like my father's
& torn innards
   like my mother's
& they both felt
   & were—
& i am a product of that—
& not a political consciousness

In "Dialogue," Parker writes: "Mother, dear mother, I'm passed/ Working my whole life away,/ Trying to join a higher class." In *Womanslaughter*, the poet is one "of the four/ daughters of Buster Cooks,/ children, survivors/ of soul-searing poverty,/ survivors of small town/ mentality, survivors." She writes, "I am a child of America/ a step child/ raised in the back room/ yet taught/ taught how to act/ in her front room." *Movement in Black* brings together class and race in its assertion of black women's presence as forgotten workers in American history:

I am the Black woman
& i have been all over
i went out west, yeah
the Black soldiers
had women too,
& i settled the land,
& raised crops & children
but that wasn't all
i hauled freight
& carried mail,
drank plenty whiskey
shot a few men too.
books don't say much
about what I did
but I was there
& i kept on moving.

The subjects of Grahn's poems as well as Parker's are ordinary things and people. Judy Grahn's *Common Woman Poems* are a sequence of seven portraits of white working class women. They include upwardly mobile, male-identified Helen; Ella, a waitress in a truck stop on Highway 80; Nadine, resting on her neighbor's stoop "counting/ rats and raising 15 children,/ half of them her own"; Carol, a closeted lesbian living a double life at work and home; Detroit Annie, flashy, exciting and self destructive; Margaret, fired for organizing a union at her workplace; and Vera, a "pale old woman" who seems beaten but isn't: "for your persistent nerve/ and plain white talk—/ the common woman is as common/ as good bread/ as common as when you couldn't go on/ but did." Finally, the *Common Woman* includes the poet, who enters the sequence in the last poem with a committed and revolutionary conclusion which formally moves the sequence from individual and objective to subjective and communal.

> For all the world we didn't know we held in common
> all along
> the common woman is as common as the best of bread
> and will rise
> and will become strong—I swear it to you
> I swear it to you on my own head
> I swear it to you on my common
> woman's
> head

These are ordinary women, angry, dangerous women, each trying to survive, to take or maintain control over her life. The portraits of these women, and the whole idea of the sequence, are set against the concept of the extraordinary woman, the uncommon woman, the token woman. The end of the poem moves from the seven individuals to a community of women, realizing the potential that had been only latent in their individual isolated situations.

The poems of Judy Grahn and Pat Parker are strong, rough, and highly crafted; they are powerful and they are often beautiful, but they are not pretty. In "The Psychoanalysis of Edward the Dyke," the title poem of her first published volume, Grahn satirically rejects the use of romantic, nonordinary language to describe her own reality as a working class lesbian. When the psycho-analyst asks Edward what homosexuality means to her, she answers: "Love flowers pearl of delighted arms. Warm and water. Melting of vanilla wafer in the pants. Pink petal roses. . . . Pastry. Gingerbread. . . . Cinnamon toast poetry. Justice equality higher wages. Independent angel song. It means I can do what I want." Adrienne Rich points out in her essay on Grahn's poetry that it is Edward's dissociation from language that would realistically describe her that finally makes her vulnerable to the behavior modification techniques of the psychoanalyst. Grahn herself re-jects in this early poem both cinnamon toast poetry and the stereotype of the decadent, upper class, cultured, wealthy, early twentieth-century (white) lesbian.[6]

I do not know if Pat Parker ever considered writing cinnamon toast poetry. I doubt it. Her poetry is performance oriented and, like the work of black feminist working class writer hattie gossett, gains shape, power, and resonance as it moves off the page. Working class poetry seems to ask for direct audience contact, for participation as well as appreciation, and in this also it is com-munal rather than individual. Pat Parker's *Movement in Black*, for example, was first performed in concert at the Oakland Audi-torium.[7] It is a story and chant which evokes the presence of black women in America in the poem's "I am" form:

> I'm the junkie with a jones
> I'm the dyke in the bar
> I'm the matron at county jail
> I'm the defendant with nothin' to say.
>
> I'm the woman with eight kids
> I'm the woman who didn't have any
> I'm the woman who's poor as sin
> I'm the woman who's got plenty.

This is not the kind of poetry that simply invites you to take it and a pocketful of apples off into a meadow to while away the after-noon. The poetry of Pat Parker and Judy Grahn, like radical poetry of any kind, turns a listener/reader back into the world rather than back into the poem. Its intent is to make its audience angry, proud, energetic. It is a means as well as an end.

The poetry is factual as well as metaphorical, direct as often as indirect. Grahn says, of *A Woman Is Talking To Death*, "Once a woman poet begins telling the truth there is no end of possibilities. This poem is as factual as I could possibly make it — a literary permission which was granted to me at the time by the work of Pat Parker" and others.[8]

> Have you ever committed any indecent acts with women?
> Yes, many. I am guilty of allowing suicidal women to
> die before my eyes or in my ears or under my hands because
> I thought I could do nothing. I am guilty of leaving a
> prostitute who held a knife to my friend's throat to
> keep us from leaving, because we would not sleep with
> her, we thought she was old and fat and ugly; I am
> guilty of not loving her who needed me; I regret
> all the women I have not slept with or comforted,
> who pulled themselves away from me for lack of some-
> thing I had not the courage to fight for, for us,
> our life, our planet, our city, our meat and potatoes,
> our love. These are indecent acts, lacking courage,
> lacking a certain fire behind the eyes, which is the
> symbol, the raised fist, the sharing of resources,
> the resistance that tells death he will starve for
> lack of the fat of us, our extra. Yes I have committed
> acts of indecency with women and most of them were acts
> of omission. I regret them bitterly.

Grahn builds on the quiet statement of facts, piles one on top of another, until their sheer weight launches her into heightened language. She says in her preface to this poem: "One characteristic of working class writing is that we often pile up many events within a small amount of space rather than detailing the many implications of one or two events. This means both that our lives are chock full of action and also that we are bursting with stories which haven't been printed, made into novels, dictionaries, philosophies."[9] Pat Parker's *Goat Child* is a list bursting with facts and events of the first 22 years of her life. In a similar fashion in a later poem Parker redefines "the law":

> the law
> comes to homes
> & takes the poor
> for traffic tickets
> the law
> takes people to jail
> for stealing food
> the law
> comes in mini-skirts
> to see if your home
> is bare enough
> for welfare
> the law
> sits in robes
> in courtrooms
> & takes away
> your children

Historically, working class poetry has been simple rather than complicated, accessible rather than obscure—the intent is to communicate clearly. There has been no particular value placed on difficulty or density; often a transparency of line replaces studied ambiguity.[10] Pat Parker and Judy Grahn inherit this tradition and modify it. Their poems are highly crafted but accessible and clear, even in the complicated task of remythologizing which Judy Grahn performs in her latest volume, *The Queen of Wands.*

> Just as, Helen, you dreamed and weaved it
> eons past, just as your seamy fingers
> manufactured so much human culture,
> all that encloses, sparks
> and clothes the nakedness of flesh and
> mind and spirit,

Helen, you always were the factory.
Helen you always were the factory.
Helen you always were the factory.
Helen you always were producer.
Helen you always were
who ever is
the weaving tree
and Mother of the people.
    ("Helen you always were/ the factory")[11]

The poetry of Judy Grahn and Pat Parker redefines hero and the heroic. In "the mock interrogation" section of A Woman Is Talking To Death which I quoted earlier, Judy Grahn redefines heroism as involvement. In Movement in Black, Parker redefines heroic to include quiet survival against odds. In her poems of self reference, Parker frequently uses the word "child": goatchild, child of myself, (step) child of America, child of the sun, daughter of dark, what kind of child is this. Her first long published poem, the epic Goat Child, tells the story of her first twenty-two years — from Houston slum to California, through marriage and to a sense of self. What does it mean to call yourself a goat child? Fear and insecurity, self dislike and not fitting in are balanced by strength, stubbornness, and a righteous anger. To refer to yourself as a child suggests vulnerability, marginality, precariousness. It also suggests the potential of growth: goat child suggests two contradictory things at once and holds the vulnerability and the strength in tension.[12]

Finally, I want to say something about the use value of this lesbian feminist working class poetry. Tannacito says of the poetry of the Colorado miners that "its real value was the immediate use made of it by its local audience of miners and sympathizers. By means of these poems the worker poets formed an intensified relationship with their worker audience that is not characteristic of twentieth-century poetry in the received canon. The miners shared an unalienated social poetry; that is, a poetry of commitment, communication, and concreteness. The poetry of the Colorado miners contributed to the mining community's definition of its common life, work, and goals."[13] Judy Grahn says of her own *Common Woman* poems that they:

> More than fulfilled my idealistic expectations of art as a useful subject—of art as a doer, rather than a passive object to be admired. All by themselves they went around the country. Spurred by the enthusiasm of women hungry for realistic pictures, they were reprinted hundreds of times, were put to music, danced, used to name various women's projects, quoted and then misquoted in a watered-down fashion for use on posters and T-shirts.[14]

Working class literature comes out of working class experience, makes a bridge between the individual and the community, is active, in the world, and meant to be used. The poetry of Pat Parker and Judy Grahn has been read or chanted at women's gatherings and, like women's music, has performed the function of bringing a group of women together. Particularly when the audience already knows the poems, the reading of them in performance has a political, ritual, sometimes spiritual function. Their use at that moment is not primarily as an occasion for individual and private appreciation of their aesthetic qualities; rather it is an occasion for the recreation of an energy flow that fosters solidarity, that connects art, politics, and everyday life. and that encourages people to continue their struggle, even if that simply means getting through the next day with integrity. The poems create, and recreate, community.

Pat Parker writes: "We as women face a particular oppression, not in a vacuum but as part of this corrupt system. The issues of women are the issues of the working class as well. By not having this understanding, the women's movement has allowed itself to be co-opted and mis-directed."[15] The poetry of Judy Grahn and Pat Parker has been read, appreciated, and of use since the late 1960s as radical feminist poetry. We need to read it also as radical working class poetry.

NOTES

[1] I agree with Mary Daly (*Gyn/Ecology: The Metaethics of Radical Feminism*, Boston: Beacon Press, 1978) and Dale Spender (*Man Made Language*, London: Routledge & Kegan Paul, 1980) that "patriarchy is everywhere." Spender goes on to say that patriarchy is "a frame of reference, a particular way of classifying and organizing the objects and events of the world; it is a form of 'order' which patterns our existence . . . [an] inclusive term to encompass a sex-class system, and a symbolic system which supports male supremacist social arrangements." (p. 4)

[2] Paul Lauter, "Working Class Women's Literature: An Introduction to Study" in *Radical Teacher* #15 (December 1979) and "Traditional and Working Class Poetry," a paper presented at the Modern Language Association Conference, December 1981; Lawrence Levine, *Black Culture and Black Consciousness: Afro-American Folk Thought from Slavery to Freedom* (Oxford: Oxford University Press, 1977); Dan Tannacito, "Poetry of the Colorado Miners, 1903-1906" in *Radical Teacher* #15 (December 1979); Martha Vicinus, *The Industrial Muse* (New York: Barnes and Noble, 1974).

[3] Judy Grahn, *The Work of a Common Woman: The Collected Poetry of Judy Grahn, 1964-1977* (Oakland, CA: Diana Press, 1978). All of Grahn's poetry quoted here, unless otherwise noted, is from this collection. Pat Parker, *Movement in Black: The Collected Poetry of Pat Parker, 1961-1978* (Oakland, CA: Diana Press, 1978). All of Parker's poetry quoted here, unless otherwise noted, is from this collection. Some of these poems are recorded: *Where Would I Be Without You, The Poetry of Pat Parker and Judy Grahn* (Olivia Records).

[4] Clearly, their poetry shows the influence of mainstream poetry, Black poetry, and feminist poetry as well. What I want to do here is point out an influence that has been overlooked. In addition, Grahn and Parker are Southwestern poets: both grew up in Texas, then moved to California.

[5] Thanks to Toni Cade Bambara for clarifying my thinking on this point.

[6] Adrienne Rich, "Power and Danger: Works of a Common Woman," in *On Lies, Secrets, and Silence* (New York: W. W. Norton, 1979), p. 252. A young lesbian writer in the early 1960s had primarily these literary role models to come to terms with: Amy Lowell, Gertrude Stein, Renée Vivien, Natalie Barney, Radclyffe Hall, Djuna Barnes. None of them was working class. The poets among them took refuge in stylistic density (Stein), "cinnamon toast poetry" (Lowell) or the French language (Vivien). Judy Grahn, in her preface to *Edward the Dyke and Other Poems*, makes peace with her literary heritage by creating "an art which

helps us see ourselves without masks." "At 16," Grahn writes, "I thought that the apex of poetic success would be to appear in the same anthology with Amy Lowell. What has actually happened is infinitely more real. . . .

"I called my first woman-produced, mimeographed book *Edward the Dyke and Other Poems*. . . . It meant people had to say the word *dyke*. What would Amy Lowell say to this? She would probably offer me a cigar." (*The Work of a Common Woman*, p. 24).

[7]by Linda Tillery, Vicki Randle, Alberta Jackson, Mary Watkins, and Pat Parker.

[8]Grahn, p. 112.

[9]Ibid., p. 112. This is also true of working class fiction. See Meridel LeSueur, *The Girl* (Cambridge, MA: West End Press, 1979); Sharon Riis, *The True Story of Ida Johnson* (Toronto: The Women's Press, 1976); Judy Grahn, ed., *True to Life Adventure Stories*, Vols. I & II. Volume I, originally published by Diana Press in 1978, was reissued by The Crossing Press in 1983. Crossing also published Vol. II in 1981.

[10]Lauter, "Traditional and Working Class Poetry," p. 8.

[11]Judy Grahn, *The Queen of Wands* (Trumansburg, NY: The Crossing Press, 1982), p. 92.

[12]For further discussion of this point, see Pamela J. Annas, "A Poetry of Survival: Unnaming and Renaming in the Poetry of Audre Lorde, Pat Parker, Sylvia Plath, and Adrienne Rich" in *Colby Library Quarterly*, Vol. XVIII, No. 1 (March 1982), pp. 9-25.

[13]Tannacito, "Poetry of the Colorado Miners, 1903-1906," pp. 1-2.

[14]Grahn, p. 60.

[15]Pat Parker, "Revolution: It's Not Neat or Pretty or Quick" in *This Bridge Called My Back: Writings by Radical Women of Color*, eds., Cherríe Moraga and Gloria Anzaldúa (Watertown, MA: Persephone Press, 1981), p. 240.

ELSA GIDLOW

CASTING A NET:
EXCERPTS FROM AN AUTOBIOGRAPHY

The dreariness of typing shipping advices eight hours a day, six and a half days a week had become barely endurable. In my despondency I was so withdrawn even from the respite of pranks and limerick-making that my work associates teased me about being in love. "Who is he?" they kept asking. And I, scornfully: "There is no *he*." The assumption, for them, was the obvious one. Into the monotony of the days they injected what relief they were able with flirting. Between the half-dozen women and the greater number of men, including those who came through with errands or requests from the yards or machine shops, there was a perpetual atmosphere of sensual potential. The two women with desks next to mine whose husbands were overseas exuded amorous need.

Blonde, blousy Mollie Simms and Nellie Pritchard, who had a plain, Cockney earthiness, in undertones while they typed bewailed having to go to bed alone. "Dribble, dribble, dribble, what do you do when there is nothing to put in there—stick something in yourself?" And Mrs. Simms, lugubriously: "What fun is that, no one behind it. My feet get cold, too, without him."

The machine shop workers who came by with their lists of needed parts sensed the sexual aura like tomcats, but in the wives, ingrained virtue of sorts and patriotic loyalty to their "fighting men" kept it all on a level of tension that was expressed mainly in ribald verbal exchanges that introduced me to new sorts of language. French-Canadian Davilla Benoit, whom I liked best, had a different approach to life's basics. Slight, dark, sinewy, widowed or divorced, she talked with unself-conscious gaiety of her lover, Jack.

Lightheartedly, she told of their nights together, whether their lovemaking had been good or not-so-good, told of their spats and making up, always with a humorous tenderness, however frank, and with no coarseness. We heard how he brought her gifts or took her out to a special dinner and theatre to win her back when he had behaved in a way to annoy her. "I just let that happen sometimes, it keeps it interesting. He always apologizes, he wants me so much. A man will do anything if he has a hard-on." She would laugh gaily, never breaking the rhythm of her expert typing: ' He knows I can't do without him either." It sounded to me so very different from marriage. In that working-class environment no one appeared disturbed by the liaison.

The specific and physical confidences of these middle-aged women were for me another sort of education, but, like so much already, I could not relate it to myself. Over Céline Drouault, also French-Canadian, the talk flowed as over snow without warming it. The pale, soft-voiced girl, maybe a year older than myself, re-iterating her felt vocation of becoming a nun, definitely was not interested in the beau they also teased her with until they ceased in the face of her unaltered tranquillity. Towards me, it was a different matter. I plainly was not convent material. ("Not with your bedroom eyes," Davilla tried laughingly to draw out confession, "I bet he loves your devilment. . . . Oh, come on, you can't hide it.")

My truthful, "I am not interested in men," made them laugh and tease the more. They did not believe me but could not make me out. They could see that I more or less ignored the men in the office beyond the necessary interchanges. I would not have rejected male companionship, but soon I decided there was not a man there with whom I could hold a conversation about anything except what was described in the shipping advices, certainly none who thought poetry or poets were important.

There was one other woman in the office, Rebecca Stuart, who aroused my curiosity. She was muscular, handsome, with a strong voice and hearty laugh. Above us in office status, she sat on a high stool at a sloping desk and did bookkeeping. She joked more with the men than with the women, but like one of them, not flirtatiously. Each day at the lunch hour she would be on the telephone for a long time, speaking low, tender-sounding, in a voice quite different from her jovial office tone and manner. When she hung up, there was a soft look in her eyes. One evening a remarkably lovely young woman with red-gold hair and a gorgeous figure (as the men's eyes attested) came to call for Rebecca. They walked out with closely linked arms pressed against one another's sides.

The following morning I could not forbear saying to Rebecca: "What glorious hair your friend has" (thinking, with pain, "like Frances").

Rebecca glowed as if I had complimented her: "Ah she's a winner."

The visitor, like a ray of glory in the drab office, had aroused envious attention from the men. It surprised me to overhear disparaging remarks about Rebecca, with whom all of them previously had seemed to be on such comradely terms. There were peculiar snickers, whispers. From one, a Scot: "Sure, and ye know, don't ye, she's a mofredite."

That was how I heard it. With all my attention to dictionaries, my widening reading and study of the encyclopedia, never had I come across such a word. I hunted now and could find nothing resembling it, although I tried various spellings. It was not until a year later, looking through a volume of photographs of ancient Greek statuary, that the word "hermaphrodite" leapt to my eyes. I realized it was of that that I must have heard an ignorant pronunciation. Putting it together with the personality of Rebecca and the leer with which the man had mouthed the word, I guessed it must have been used as a slur on the woman's supposed masculinity. Something to puzzle over the more—until nearly a year later I took a step that catapulted me into a more sophisticated human environment.

Before then there were months of dejected aching, in body and heart and with fury of mind at what appeared to me as sordid grown-up life. I felt myself at some extremity, like the mouse dropped by what malevolence or chance into the carton, in darkness and frustration, struggling to climb the sides. At that point, two resolutions were born, written and underlined in the journal I kept spasmodically: *I am going to get a room of my own. I am going to find my kind of people.*

The resolve was made, like casting a net blind into unknown waters. How bait Fate's hook? The seventy-five dollars a month had looked large. When I calculated paying the rent and supporting myself entirely, it shrank to nothing, especially as I was sharing it at home to help Mother. I wished to continue doing that. The impossibility of going to college, lacking both money and the preliminary schooling, had to be accepted. It must be added that I lacked also the bodily robustness that can make obstacles and hardships no more than incentive to overcome them. Since none of us went to doctors or had physical examinations when I was young, I did not learn until years later that my heart was not strong. The colds, bronchitis, influenza that plagued me were treated with home remedies or ignored and taken for granted. Survival had always required a stoicism of which Mother was a prime example. There was no model or encouragement for self-pity. What happened was the human condition.

But let us bless books, poets, artists, music-makers of all sorts. As I found greater access to them, they taught me that drabness, tedium, injustice were not the whole of life, that there were worlds of high-hearted realities, of spiritual transcendence. No angels with flaming swords were guarding entrance to those worlds against those who dared the adventure of claiming citizenship.

The young, and maybe their elders as well, tend to believe that what they seek is somewhere else. It was my faith then that if I could travel I should begin to discover the wider life, the more challenging and rewarding experiences, the people informed by wisdom and love of beauty that reading convinced me existed. Today, the imagination of the young bounds out into space for realization of a science-fiction sort of fantasy. Earlier, in the United States, it was continental exploration and down-to-earth pioneering that fed imagination. I am of the sea-going English and of an earlier generation when oceans were the perilous, little known routes to ports of glamour. Ships and seas were always the content of my dreams.

The fall of the year was and is my most restless time, as if I have in me some urge to seasonal migration. One autumn day of special desperation and aloneness, I said to Davilla Benoit as we ate our sandwich lunch, "I am going to run away to sea." Of course that was very funny for a girl. She simply smiled. I knew that this expedient for exploring the great beckoning world, open to moneyless young men, was denied to me because of my sex. Yet so persistently did it haunt my imagination that I thought of cutting off my hair, wearing male garb and "signing on" as cabin boy on a ship bound for any port of Orient or Antipodes. Simply to be sailing the unknown seas was lure enough, they were so much in my night dreams. Jeer at my romantic, ignorant projecting and tell me I should first explore my own inner ocean. I was doing that too, though holding the feeling that Life with a capital L was "out there."

Hallowe'en came. My sisters, brother Stanley and I always had devised masks and costumes to go masquerading with our pumpkin lanterns on All Hallows' Eve. This year I let them go alone. Stanley, though younger, had caught up with me in height. His clothes would just about fit me. I borrowed some old ones, wound and pinned my abundant hair up tightly, stuffed it into a cap of Father's and went bare-faced to call on Davilla. It thrilled me that a black-eyed French girl on the streetcar kept looking at me as if flirting. I was too shy to do more than smile.

Davilla laughed heartily when she realized I was seriously considering the adventure I had threatened. "Whether the captain thinks he sees a girl or a pretty boy, *he* will quickly discover for himself a delightful adventure. You will not very long be a virgin."

That possibility—rape—had not occurred to me. With discouragement I listened as Davilla took me to her tall mirror. "Look—your delicate figure—hands—lady's hands, so pretty— eyes—you think a young man would have such a mischievous smile?—and your voice! *Ma petite*, you may not be born to make babies—I am not, either, but you are all woman. You cannot deceive."

I had to admit that, although I might appear a bit boyish, there was nothing masculine about me. I never had wanted to be male, only to be free to do things men could do. Now I know there have been not a few women who dared the male masquerade to achieve the freedom they were denied, many succeeding life-long, but they may have been more convincingly male-featured. I was forced to admit the impossibility of getting on a ship to dis-cover wider, more shining horizons—for the present at least, until I could buy a ticket. But I would not be defeated. I devised a bait and cast my net into nearer unknown waters to bring to me what I might not yet go in search of.

In the late autumn of 1917, a letter appeared in the people's col-umn of the *Montreal Daily Star.* It inquired if any group or organi-zation of writers and artists existed in the city which a person seriously interested in such pursuits might join. There was no reply, but a little more than a week later a second letter appeared responding to the first. It stated that a group of writers was being formed, and suggested that the inquirer and any other interested should "communicate with the undersigned at the address given."

Both letters were written by that lonely young woman groping towards her kind, the first under a pseudonym. Over the course of a week I received nearly a dozen replies from individuals of both sexes asking for information about the proposed group. I invited them all to a meeting at my parents' on an evening when Father would be away, telling Mother what I was doing. With the help of my sister Thea, who was also interested, I made the little parlour as tidy and attractive as I could, bought flowers, asked Mother if she would bake some sweet buns and added a bottle of port wine.

An odd assortment of people came, all declaring interest in writing except one gentle-mannered Jew who said he was a painter. A large, blonde, lame woman was helped up the two flights of steps to our flat by her husband, who left saying he would return for her at ten. She was crippled with arthritis, passed her time writing and trying to sell short stories to women's magazines. There was a pretty, freckled, red-haired girl, Edith Strachan, not much older than myself, who had won prizes for writing at school. A man in a lieutenant's uniform from some other part of Canada diffidently confided he thought his experiences in the war might be exciting to write about when he returned from fighting to save democracy. Doris Reid also came with her husband, who left her there and departed; originally from England, she had lived in India. A number of middle-aged men came primarily hoping to find amorous companionship, attracted by the female name signed to the second letter. The one exception was Alfred Gordon; he arrived with a fat sheaf of typewritten verse which he said would come out as a book when he had collected the retail price of its publication from two hundred sponsors. He was ready with sign-up sheets and promised to honour us with a reading later in the evening.

The most astonishing of all was a being of elegance and beauty, a willowy blond: "God made him for a man so let him pass as such," Gordon quoted in sibilant *sotto voce* to the lieutenant. The anomalous being ("Roswell George Mills," he announced himself, "of the *Montreal Star*") overheard Gordon's quotation from Shakespeare and gave him a supercilious stare. The remark was spiteful and uncalled-for. I could not blame its target for as spiteful a retaliation when the opportunity arose. At the point in the evening when Gordon proposed starting his reading, Mills vetoed it and won support from the rest. "Let's get to know one another first. We are not, I assume, gathered here to begin by boring one another to death."

R G Mills of the *Star*, the shy Scottish girl, Edith, the Jewish artist whose name was Gershon Benjamin, Mrs Reid from India and possibly the poet, Gordon, were the only members of the group who appeared promising. All the middle-aged men left early, put off by the indifference to their advances of the two young women and bored by talk of writing techniques. The lieutenant, who obviously could barely contain his horror and distaste for Mills, failed to show up at the next meeting, scheduled for Mills's home (he lived with his parents).

The arthritic woman, Maisie McBane, arrived faithfully at all of the weekly gatherings, escorted by her husband until he rebelled. Then she appealed to Edith or me to pick her up at her home in an outlying part of the city and help her on and off the streetcars. All of us found her tiresome, her sentimental stories boring, her conventional attitudes a restraint on conversation. For a time I acquiesced, without enthusiasm, to the demand for escort service. It meant I had to rush home from work and bolt dinner without a moment's pause. The McBane's house was more than half an hour by streetcar, forty minutes from there to the Mills's where we most often gathered. One night I rebelled and told a lie. "I am not feeling very well," I told her on the telephone. "I don't think I'll be going."

When I arrived at the meeting, Roswell said, "Thank God she's not coming. I was getting ready to shock the wits out of her by announcing I should like to make love to her son. Did you know she has a quite good-looking boy of seventeen or so? I met them on the street one Saturday. Now if she would have *him* bring her. . . ."

The doorbell rang. It was Mrs McBane. She stared at me and turned chilly. "I thought you weren't coming."

Feeling badly that she would guess now we did not want her, I tried to salve the situation. "I was tired after a hard day's work, but took a rest and felt better, so I came anyway."

Maisie, looking aggrieved, eased herself into the most comfortable armchair, reposing her cane at her feet, muttering that young people no longer cared to help a poor crippled woman. Roswell, floating past her to the kitchen, sweetly asked, "Did your son bring you? He is such a *pretty* boy. I'd like to know him."

Maisie turned red. "*There* is a *vicious* young man. I am coming to the conclusion I do not belong here." She left early, refusing tea which Edith passed around with the cake Roswell had made. To our surprise, she managed nicely alone, limping out and down the stairs with the aid of her cane. Roswell turned from watching her through the living-room curtains. "Do you realize she came here without help and is leaving the same way? It a-Maisies me she has the gall to expect you to go all the way out to Westmount to fetch her and take her back." There was laughter and a couple of groans at his pun. But I still felt badly, both about the lie and having hurt the woman's feelings, although I was convinced I had been justified. With fiercely youthful intolerance I burst out, "People should not be boring and ugly and pitiable, making others feel like beasts for not catering to them." It was the last we saw of her.

Gradually a wide variety of individuals joined us: musicians, medical students, painters, amateur actors and some out-of-work professional, but interesting, men. At last I had found people I could enjoy, converse with, learn from and perhaps love. The most interesting to me was Roswell. He was only nineteen, but older in his mind and in experience. Conscious also of being an "outsider" and of the need to compensate for it, he worked hard despite his languid manner. His main interest was music; he took piano lessons and practised tirelessly to a ticking metronome. His job on the *Star* was assisting the editor of the financial page. On the side he conducted a lovelorn column where, cynical tongue in cheek, he gave very proper counsel under a female name. And he found time to write music and drama criticism, which brought him free passes to the city's cultural events. To some of these he took me when there was no likely young man to court or impress. I thus enjoyed my first concerts, operas, theatrical productions, to which I could rarely have afforded tickets. A marvellous new world opened.

Besides these events and people, Roswell also introduced me to a whole new range of literature I might not so quickly have discovered, along with the lives of its makers: Oscar Wilde and Alfred Douglas, Baudelaire, Verlaine, Mallarmé, Swinburne, Maeterlinck, Max Beerbohm, Joris Karl Huysmans. All were bourgeois-scorning, "decadent" rebels of the Nineties and early Twenties with their glamorous sinfulness or metaphysical retreat from unendurable middle-class living. Haunting libraries, I made discoveries of my own: Nietzsche, whose *Thus Spake Zarathustra* transported me to delirious heights of recognition; de

Quincy's *Confessions of an English Opium Eater* which roused in me a desire to make like experiments. When I found small brown tablets of opium among Father's first-aid supplies, I stole some and hid them away for later experimentation. I studied French by myself on streetcars so as to be able to read in the original Baudelaire's *Les Fleurs du Mal,* excited to find him writing of love, passionate love, between women.

Roswell confided to me his personal crusade. He wanted people to understand that it was beautiful, not evil, to love others of one's own sex and make love with them. Roswell had divined my lesbian temperament and was happy to proselytize; the veil of self-ignorance began to lift. Together we read Havelock Ellis's *Psychology of Sex,* and other such volumes (available mainly to the medical profession) as we were able to get our hands on. We read Edward Carpenter's *The Intermediate Sex* and his *Towards Democracy.* I still have a copy of that thin India paper volume, much marked.

A new member of our group, Louis Gross, a graduate medical student from McGill University, helped us to get access to some of the forbidden books. He introduced us to Krafft-Ebing, Guy Lombroso, who argued that "genius" was decadent, to Freud and Albert Einstein. Try to grasp how explosive all of this was to a young mind in 1916. I began to look for books on psychology to seek deeper understanding of why I had always felt myself an "outsider" in ordinary life.

Roswell developed an unrequited love for the young medical student who did not walk the lavender path, and lamented to me at length of his sufferings. He relieved them writing plays celebrating erotic love between men, in the mood of Maeterlinck. He wrote of the tragedy inherent in the scorn and persecution with which this love was met by a crass society. The trial and jailing of Oscar Wilde were not far in our past and very real. We read his *Ballad of Reading Gaol. Tragedies of Sex* by Frank Wedekind was another of the books that instructed us in the cruelties of society to those who did not walk in its prescribed paths.

In response to Roswell's confidences about his unhappy love

live, I in turn told him of the feelings I had had for Frances. I
spoke of her "betrayal," now recognizing that I had been "in
love." At this point Roswell told me of Sappho. I went searching
for all I could find of her translated fragments, not much, and anything written about her, also scarce at the time. Instead of accepting society's rejection, we two iconoclasts rejected our rejectors,
proud to be the spiritual and passional kin of Sappho, the Shakespeare of the Sonnets, Jesus, Michelangelo, Leonardo da Vinci,
Carpenter, Walt Whitman, and hundreds more of the world's admired individuals whose secret lives we ferreted out from forbidden chronicles. We delved into the mores of ancient Greece, read
Plato's dialogues, dreamed of an ideal society as we studied his
Republic. In all of this and more we found reasons for loving ourselves and each other.

I thought Roswell was the most ambiguously beautiful being I
knew, with his metallic blond hair and pale, perfect features, his
languidly intelligent grey eyes and soft, slim body; his was a hot-
house beauty, like a living flower that appeared artificial. He
went scrubbed in tweeds to his work on the newspaper, but at
home among friends, at the theatre and concerts, he was deli-
cately made-up and elegantly dressed, wearing exotic jewelry
and as colorful clothes as he dared. Receiving at home, he
donned a bronze green robe of heavy silk. He gently maintained
that it was necessary to startle the bourgeoisie, not for the sake of
shocking but to shake them out of their smugness, make them
realize they were half alive and doing their best to destroy all who
did not fit into their mould. "Greasy domesticity" was not godly
but a blight. In one way or another, every generation repeats such
revolt. Older men had been Roswell's mentors when he was
younger. I also was grateful to them for helping to open up the
worlds of thought and art.

I inquired one day how Roswell had escaped being drawn into
the maw of war. "Oh, I'm Four-F — physically, mentally, emotion-
ally and morally incompetent for the glory of killing," he explained.
Mabel, his mother, was most relieved not to have borne a soldier.
"My father can't stand the sight of me; it's mutual. He's in the last

stages of alcoholism: cirrhosis of the liver, poor idiot. No wonder Mabel couldn't endure it any longer and took a lover."

I had seen the man who was Mabel's lover and imagined him to be a relative of some sort. Mabel was as beautiful as her son, with the same colouring but voluptuous and healthy like one of Titian's women. She dressed smartly; her son helped design her clothes. They were more like elder sister and brother than mother and son and went out a lot together. They shared cosmetics. She accepted him as he was.

Wishing to add sophistication to my unassuming appearance, Roswell designed for me a draped, goddess-like, close-fitting evening dress, which I sewed. He suggested I carry a calla lily with it when we went to concerts or receptions of friends together. I balked at that Wildean extravagance. He also tried to persuade me to use make-up, but I could not be bothered. It was fun occasionally to "dress up" for a dramatic appearance, but generally I was too preoccupied with writing. I preferred to be admired for my mind and what it could accomplish. "One can also be beautiful," he argued. "You didn't even know you had beautiful hands, the most beautiful I have seen." He wrote poetry to them and other supposed charms.

Some of the other young men also were flattering. Gershon, the painter, said I was beautiful and he wished to paint me. Louis, a sculptor, told me, "You have a Burne-Jones body and a Rossetti neck," reciting Dante Gabriel Rossetti's lines: "The blessed damozel leaned out/ From the gold bar of heaven. . . ."

Roswell gave me the pet name of Sappho ("You are strong and independent like her and a true poet"). The others picked it up and it was my name among them for years until I left Montreal. All heady and romantic—but I knew I was not pretty; there was nothing remarkable about my appearance. "No, you are not pretty, thank God," Roswell said, "but you are an individual. Make the most of it. Learn how to dress. I'll help you." The situation at least was pleasant and added to my self-confidence.

Roswell and I became inseparable, feeling, if not altogether knowing why, that we complemented one another, loving with a pure, Platonic love. His gender ambiguity both attracted me and left me feeling safe. I was constantly defending him to people, mainly men, who regarded him as corrupt. He could have a viper's tongue against those he disliked, against smugness and persons who went out of their way to insult him, as was not infrequent, but I knew him for a loyal, gentle and generous friend, one to whom I already owed a great deal and was to owe more. Our friendship was to be lifelong.

Fascinating fish my homemade net had caught. Whatever contributed to my devising remains unanalyzable. But from that action in a desperate moment I learned never to tolerate stagnation. Even in the most deprived circumstances it is possible to proclaim: "I am here, world: where are you? What do you want of me?"

The rest of my life depended on the threads of that innocently cast net.

MONIKA KEHOE

THE MAKING OF A DEVIANT*

[*After finishing her Ph.D. in language and literature from Ohio State in 1935, Monika hoped to obtain a Doctor of Divinity degree from the Pontifical Institute in Toronto. When it rejected her application because she was a woman, she felt strangely separated from Roman Catholicism. But because of the scarcity of jobs in those Depression years, she accepted a teaching position at a Catholic women's college in a large Midwestern city, where the lay faculty lived in cells like those of the nuns. After a month of this austerity, when Monika requested permission to live off campus, the college president warned her not to invite students to her apartment. "Her perceptive appraisal of the possibilities rather startled me. She was obviously more worldly-wise than any of the nuns I had known before."*

Almost immediately, Monika fell in love with a senior at the college, Helen, and then had to write "I'm sorry but it's all over" notes to two lovers form her undergraduate days who were planning to join her in the big city. By the time Helen graduated, Monika wanted a job at a secular college, so the two women set off for California in the summer of 1936. All their belongings were packed in Monika's car; a used Ford phaeton with a collapsible canvas top. Ed.]

In 1936, overnight accommodation at many motor "courts" was 50¢, if you brought your own sheets. The entire cost for our hop to the coast that summer, including gas and oil, was less than fifty dollars.

It had been eight years since my European tour which was the last vacation I had had. After that I had spent seven consecutive years in uninterrupted schooling—four as an undergraduate and

---

*Excerpt from Chapter 5, "Pedagogue."

three as a graduate student. I had taken full course loads every summer, as well as during the regular sessions. I had to, in order to retain my scholarship. Now, I had just completed my first year of teaching under heavy stress. I was twenty-six and I thought I was burned out. I really needed a holiday and a change of scenery.

Two or three incidents stand out in my memory of that two-week drive. All were the result of what must have been my strange appearance—my "epicene proclivities," as one of my more articulate critics later described it—my custom of flaunting convention, something I was quite oblivious of at the time. The first was a rather frightening experience of being asked to leave a tiny town in Nebraska where we had stopped at a general store to buy some cold ham for lunch. We seldom ate in restaurants; they were not part of our economy plan. We were, I recall, dressed in shorts; it was a hot day. The town marshal or sheriff met me on the steps of the store to tell me that my attire was indecent.

"Either you get some clothes on or you mosey out of here. We don't want your kind in this town." He had a shiny badge pinned to his left breast pocket and he chewed tobacco which he spat out of the side of his mouth, much as the cowboys did in the B-grade Westerns. The next shocker happened in the evening, a few days later, when I walked into the rest room of a gas station and a woman screamed. I had on sailor pants and a pea jacket to match, an outfit I thought quite jaunty and appropriate for touring through the Rockies. When I asked her what was the matter, and she recognized I was not a man, she apologized, saying something almost inaudible about the poor lighting in the place.

As we got farther West, we wore jeans in the daytime with sneakers. I bought a Borcelino porkpie hat which Helen said looked sharp with my new cowboy boots that I began to wear most of the time instead of the sneakers. Their high heels gave me quite a lift and I tried to walk like William S. Hart. The next Sunday we stopped at a village church where some kind of a fiesta was in progress. They were obviously going to serve food after the religious service so, being hungry, we knelt on the prie-dieu behind the last pew where we wouldn't be noticed—we thought. After the altar boys with their swinging censers had passed and the bells stopped ringing, I felt a hand on my shoulder. I turned around and an elderly priest motioned toward my hat. When I didn't respond promptly as he expected, he stooped over and whispered: "Remove your hat in church." I did what I was told and he hobbled away apparently satisfied. Such incidents left me unperturbed. I was already used to being stared at as different but I didn't care. I never wanted to be like everyone else.

The next four years confirmed me in the androgynous life style that society frowned upon. They were spent at a West coast women's college where Helen took a secretarial job and I carried another heavy teaching load. The first year was again difficult. We had to live "in residence," a euphemism for dormitory accommodation, and learn to keep up a pretense of being "roommates" which probably fooled nobody. But at least at Oak Hill there was no check-in time for faculty or staff and we had our own keys. Nor were we required to attend chapel. It was my first real freedom from religion. But near the end of that year, the bad news came. Sr. Gretchen had died of a heart attack. I was crushed. Sister Gretchen, my literature professor, had been my mentor all through college. She had been more than that—a spiritual lover who had encouraged me to persist when graduate school seemed impossible. On days that were bleak with waiting for news from the university, she brought me pieces of cake or fruit from the convent refectory at lunchtime. She carried them across the campus, tucked up in the wide sleeves of her habit, while I waited in her office like a hungry puppy, greedy for a biscuit and the affection that came with it.

With the sudden death of Sister Gretchen, I felt a loss I had never known before. The last restraining influence on what she called my "wild ways"—although she never knew their extent—was gone.

By my second year at Oak Hill, I was able to build a small cabin in the nearby canyon at a cost equal to my salary for one year, or $2,000.00—a lot of money then. The site I had chosen was convenient to the college and had the virtue of being located in a section that boasted Henry Miller as one of its residents. On a neighborly visit that we made as soon as it was seemly, I was able to see, for the first time, some of the original Blake prints I had heard so much about in graduate school. Although no match for the Huntington Library collection, the Miller pictures were a dazzling surprise and I was proud to own property in their vicinity.

Planning and designing our house, then watching the redwood structure take shape, filled every day with anticipation. The interior of knotty pine, the fireplace, the half-door, the built-in bunk beds and desk—all were innovations that the contractor advised against. He said that such irregularities would reduce the resale value of the property. Resale! We would live in that house forever. The rustic view from the ceiling-to-floor windows would always be ours. Helen loved it almost as much as I did. She supervised the furnishings—picking out the denim material we liked for the drapes and bedspreads and choosing the kitchen ware and the linens. Most of the stuff we were able to buy practically new at Goodwill stores or other thrift shops in the city. The only furniture we needed, since even the dinette was built in, was a couch and a couple of easy chairs for the living room. The set we chose, of rustic unfinished wood, with the bark still on, fit in perfectly with the rest of the decor but needed cushions to avoid snagging people's clothes.

We stained the exterior of the house ourselves and waxed the interior walls. We didn't want to paint over the arabesque grain of the wood, a decoration in itself. The stain and wax just brought out its intricate design and mellow color. Above the fireplace, along the edge of the mantle, I carved the words "Red Branch House," from *Cuchulain*. I had just discovered the ancient Gaelic epic, which I had been reading in Lady Gregory's translation, and thought—indeed, still think—that it rivals Homer in elegance and beauty. Our redwood cabin was a true Red Branch House so this would be its name.

The place belonged to me legally so that I paid the bills and was the more economy-minded. Helen contributed her labor which included all the housekeeping chores and was more than her share. We lived there for exactly two years before I got hopelessly entangled with another woman, Doris, who was a graduate student at Oak Hill, and Helen moved out in disgust.

Such entanglements seem to be inevitable in academe, especiall in women's college settings. The student-teacher relationship as in the film *Liana* promotes what used to be called "crushes." This was probably intensified in the laid-back atmosphere of the college swimming pool where we basked in the California sun. It was there, stretched out on our towels, that Doris and I first talked.

It is difficult, at this distance in time, to recollect what I thought then about the moral question of lesbianism. I was no longer a Catholic and viewed sin as a culturally relative concept. "Situational ethics" is, I believe, the descriptive phrase now used for what was then my point of view. I was almost completely unaware of feminism as a political movement. I had heard of the "suffragettes" but I had absorbed the conventional view that they were ridiculous. At that stage, at the beginning of the forties, I would never have connected feminism with lesbianism anyway. Feminism was relatively respectable while homosexuality was supposed to be equivalent to insanity. The Church condemned it as a mortal sin and most people abhorred it as "unnatural."

I blocked the entire issue from my mind, refusing to think about it, and continued to feel comfortable only in the role I had come to assume. I couldn't identify with women—faculty wives, for instance. I always tried to avoid them at college gatherings. They were such sad sacks with nothing to talk about but babies and cooking or other domestic trivialities. It was as if I feared their paltriness would rub off on me. I did not perceive myself as female nor did I want any part of femininity. I wanted to be human; to be strong and lithe, not petite or pretty. My image of myself was boyish not mannish. I wished I were taller, say five-feet-ten. I abhorred the Hollywood polarization of masculine and feminine and was drawn, instead, to male hermaphroditic types and tomboy girls. I coveted what contemporary feminist psychologists would call the androgynous personality—what popular advertising mistakenly labels "unisex."

Although I admired grace in sports above all else, I never associated it with female performance. There was no Olga or Nadia then. Nor had Babe Didrikson yet surfaced. The women I knew who played tennis, at the college or at the local club, were uniformly awkward and poorly coordinated. I preferred to play with men. When tournament time came, I was in trouble. I refused to play mixed doubles, thus alienating many potential opponents, and, of course, I did not enter the women's events. I had done that once, during my undergraduate days, and vowed it would be the last. A bosomy wench in pigtails, with bows on them, had softballed me to death in the finals of a local tournament. I wasn't about to let that happen again. To me there was no glory in winning from women and it was a disgrace to lose to them. Wives of the men I liked to play with often resented my attitude, which I did not take the trouble to conceal, and they prevailed upon their husbands not to play with me. Sports, I must confess, had been almost the only area in which I can honestly say that I have personally suffered discrimination.

Generally I have been able to escape other situations which might have led to discrimination. Much of the time I may have been oblivious to it. I know now that all the misogynistic literature I read in preparation for my doctoral degree left my consciousness unraised. I usually agreed that the women characters were as foolish or as evil as they were depicted and deserved their sorry end. I never saw myself in them nor did I see through the universal design to denigrate them. I was unmindful of their depreciation because I was not one of them. In fact I had nothing but contempt for anything feminine.

At about the time that Helen moved out, the famous novelist and Blake critic Helen C. White, a staunch Roman Catholic, came to our campus from Madison. As the member of the English department who had suggested she be invited to Oak Hill, I was responsible for meeting her on arrival and seeing her to the hotel where her lodging had been arranged. The evening after her lecture, I took her for a drive along the ocean. What I remember most vividly about our brief time together was the decisive way she lifted my hand from her knee as I rested it there for a moment, quite innocently, for conversational emphasis. She was clearly not one to brook familiarities. I have often wondered, since, if this remarkably gifted woman was acutely perceptive or if I imagined her action as a rebuff.

Although Doris often stayed overnight after I was again alone in the house, she couldn't move in because she had to keep up the appearance of being a resident student. Her family called long-distance from Philadelphia, weekly, so that she didn't dare be off-campus every time they phoned.

Besides, transferring to my house would have caused more raised eyebrows at the college. Students as well as faculty were already beginning to talk. One of my colleagues made a rather sly remark about my offering such a convenient student hostel near campus. As the youngest faculty member in a fairly stuffy academic environment, I was naturally popular with the students and turned to them for my social life. This did not endear me to my colleagues. Although I didn't really care what they thought, I did care about the job.

I realized that I had to be more careful. I noted, too, that I was no longer being asked by the Dean to chaperone ski groups for weekends at the college lodge in the mountains. It was there that I had been introduced to skiing, a sport that was to become an important part of my life. On one of the Oak Hill mid-winter outings, the girls had insisted I try a pair of lumberman's nine-foot "boards" and accompany them on their "run" to the post office. The huge skis, the custodian's, were the only extra pair available. In the late thirties, before safety bindings, a heel clamp attached to a small spring was the common device used to hold the boot (or shoe) to the ski. My initiation to the sport was without any such fancy equipment. The custodian's pair had only canvas straps which fitted across the instep of my hiking boots. Thus I had no control of the skis whatever. No wonder I was slow to be converted to the sport. It was not until ten years later that I had proper boots and donned my first pair of Heads equipped with downhill safety bindings.

Just before Christmas in 1940, about the time that the new college contracts were to be issued, I received a note asking me to visit the Dean's office. This was enough of an oddity to make me apprehensive, but I was stunned, when I got there, to discover that Helen, whom I trusted completely, had told the Dean all about our relationship. As a result of her disclosure, the President had decided my contract was not to be renewed.

The Dean, who spoke frankly, pointed out that, being the elder of the two, as well as a professional person, I was the responsible half of the affair. Furthermore, the college must consider its reputation, she pointed out. No students were to visit my house for the remainder of the academic year under threat of "appropriate action" being taken against me. I have often wondered what would have constituted "appropriate action" that would not have involved more bad publicity for the institution. However, at the time, I was so intimidated that I would have agreed to anything. In fact I even agreed to consult with the local parish priest who served as chaplain for the Catholic girls enrolled at Oak Hill. I figured my academic career was over. What had happened, I was sure, would follow me for the rest of my life, wherever I might apply to teach.

The session with the Reverend was an exercise in evasion. A young man, he was more embarrassed than I and even less familiar with the vocabulary of "female perversion." We talked around the subject while he drummed the desk and I sat slumped in a chair opposite, wondering what made him tick. Finally, he concluded that I should "pray for salvation." I left feeling sick to my stomach with apprehension.

Now that I look back on this miserable interlude in my life, I am quite sure that the Dean, who had a marked resemblance to Amelia Earhart, and was a favorite among the "girls" as well, was herself a suppressed lesbian and probably projected onto me her own fears of disclosure.

Only one colleague, the chair of the philosophy department, a middle-aged woman who shared a home near the campus with a much older female professor of mathematics (both were distinguished academics with tenure) seemed able, or dared, to give me any emotional support. But even this was never expressed verbally. No allusion was ever made to the presumed cause of my separation from the college. However, I was invited to spend a great deal of time at their house, where I had lunch or tea, and was even allowed to stay one night in their guest bedroom. The entire matter was treated as if it were some unspeakable affliction which we understood had set us apart but could not be mentioned.

After I recovered from the initial shock of losing my job at Oak Hill, I got mad. I looked around for some means of revenge. By a fortunate coincidence, a distant "cousin," a Notre Dame graduate I had known since our teens, turned up for a visit. He had gotten my address from my mother and, so long as he was in the area, he doubtless thought he would stop in for a little free hospitality.

When I told him my story, Jim admitted to being a homosexual himself and said that he, too, was involuntarily unemployed, having recently been fired from his civil service post in Washington on the same charge. We found enormous comfort in our common "difference" and spent hours discussing whether or not we were crazy or the world was off its trolley. We decided in our favor and hit on a brilliant idea for recouping society's approval, to our mutual benefit. We announced our engagement. It was a real lark! The college was flabbergasted. It jumped at the chance to improve its own image which it saw as badly tarnished by the threatened scandal it had just evaded.

Various relieved administrators gave showers for Jim and me and we accumulated a large number of expensive electric appliances, cut-glass monstrosities, embroidered pillowcases and valuable bric-a-brac of all shapes and sizes. We had enough ash trays to supply the Hilton chain of hotels. Much of the stuff we promptly returned to the stores that we could identify as the source of their purchase, where we collected refunds sufficient to live on through the rest of the summer until my house was sold. Meanwhile, I applied to the Canadian Air Force which was then recruiting civilian women for war-work overseas. As soon as the sale of the house and furnishings was completed, I left for Ottawa and Jim went off to join the Marines. The WACS had not yet been organized or I would have enlisted—anything to escape the confines of the college campus.

MARY MEIGS

THE MEDUSA HEAD*

An unpredictable alchemy changes hate into love without warn-
ing, just as surely as it changes love into hate. It is as though each
is held in suspension in the other, though one would swear, when
in a love-state, that there is no atom of hate in its composition,
and vice versa. I have friends who claim to be incapable of
hating, just as they claim never to have wished someone dead. I
have friends who have loved and hated me. "I could find it in my
heart to wish you dead," wrote one whom I had hurt by writing to
her about a new love. The knowledge that I, who thought myself
so sensitive, should by my insensitivity have caused a friend to
wish me dead, was very painful. Thoughtlessness of this kind is a
cliché; one forgets that a person who feels unloved has the naked
vulnerability and the ferocity that goes with it. It is partly because
every nerve is quivering and aching and because one's heart
seems to be as drained and barren as an empty swimming pool
that love can come flooding into it with special violence. So it was
with my falling in love with Andrée, which happened without my
even seeing her, in the period between Marie-Claire's return
from Paris and Andrée's first visit to Wellfleet. Perhaps it happened even before Marie-Claire got back, for I remember listening to her saga after she arrived without rancor or the surging
assertion of ego. Every detail of her ten days with Andrée came
out in effervescent, rainbow-colored narrative which continued
for days, and in which I shared just as I was supposed to, laughing delightedly and longing to hear more. She had discovered
two Andrées: one who needed to be saved from the mournful self
who hated worldly life in general and Paris life in particular, and
one who thrived on the very same life and sparkled like a child on

---

*Excerpt from Part II.

Christmas morning in the presence of her aristocratic friends. Marie-Claire adored Andrée's contradictions and the delicious sexual avidity which she later saw as perverse. She even looked with bemused tenderness at her outbursts of bad temper, her bullying of her son, her scornful remarks about her daughter. And this accepting attitude lingered for a long time: after she had encouraged me to share the friend she loved; after I, too, was bewitched; after the friend had taken me without thanks, with, instead, a series of violent kicks in Marie-Claire's direction. Even then, when Marie-Claire saw that at times I detested the forms that Andrée's jealousy took, she would take me apart (and this was extremely difficult to do, given Andrée's watchfulness) and say, "Tu l'aimes toujours, n'est-ce pas?" pleading with me to try to understand Andrée, her suffering at the hands of cruel and loveless parents, the frustrations that explained her difficult character; in short, to see Andrée as she saw herself.

Pliable, porous cells of the other implanting themselves, changing our nature for a while, the work of love. Andrée and I began writing each other letters couched in the delicate language of flirtation, of mutual seduction, like the fluttering of two butterflies. Her handwriting suited these arabesques—it was fine and illegible, written in faint brown ink on Japanese paper, so that I spent joyful hours deciphering first the words and then the exquisite mysteries of what she was saying, with Marie-Claire, expert from long practice, helping me. She had negotiated the time of Andrée's first visit, and we drove to Boston on a cold, grey November day to meet her. She was wearing the clothes I recognized from our meeting in Paris, her face was pink and radiant. She and Marie-Claire embraced, and I remember her looking at me over Marie-Claire's shoulder just before she threw herself into my open arms with wordless joy. When we got to the house in Wellfleet, to her room back of the kitchen, she suddenly toppled backwards on the bed, and laughing, I fell, too, and we embraced each other with the greedy exuberance of people who realize that they are in love. After a few seconds I got to my feet, suddenly ill at ease, for Marie-Claire was standing motionless with, for the first time, a little smile of pure anguish on her face. It was the beginning of her dark night of the soul, precipitated by the noble observance of her belief in sharing, which is so much more difficult in fact than in theory. And in this case, it was impossible, for having fastened her attention on me with the fierce entirety of one born under the sign of Aries, Andrée had nothing left for Marie-Claire but impatience, neglect, and placating crumbs. Of the instant failure of our triangular love-making I shall only say that it helped me to discover how ruthless Andrée's exclusive nature could be. I suffered from the many forms of this ruthlessness and Andrée was angry because I suffered, but it did not prevent me from tormenting Marie-Claire with the spectacle of my love for Andrée, or make me rush to her defence every time Andrée was cruel to her. Our situation was complicated by the fact that she loved Andrée more truly and wholly than I did, for my little reservations, those she sought so hard to overcome, began almost immediately. To her, love is a work of diligent understanding, total acceptance and self-sacrifice, all of which, practised for a long term, build up demonic forces in anyone who is not a saint. Marie-Claire, in love, becomes utterly helpless and hurtable, and for Andrée the temptation to make a victim of someone who stretched herself out so willingly on the sacrificial altar, was overwhelming. It is surprising, perhaps, that I, who was loved by Andrée, turned against her sooner than Marie-Claire, who was her victim. For Marie-Claire, to be treated badly is one of the ordeals that tests love's fidelity and fans its dying embers. "*J'ai été très digne, très noble,*" she says of herself after a love-ordeal, and I admire her ability to make herself into one of her own heroines. As for her backlashes, they have the force of Joshua trumpeting down the walls of Jericho. But perhaps Marie-Claire's endless patience, her blindness to the defects of the woman she loves until she judges that she has been betrayed, come from her wish to keep her self-image inviolate by clinging to the ideal image of the beloved. The self-image is fixed in rigid relation to that of the beloved, so that a threat to one is a threat to the other. That lovers do not always behave according to the ideal seems to come as a shock to Marie-

Claire, who prefers to accept their explanations until the final Judgement Day, when the blinders fall from her eyes, and she suffers the pain, not of having been wrong, but of having loved too totally.

From the time that my nature was changed by love, Marie-Claire suffered acutely and gladly, for her own love demanded this of her. It demanded, unfortunately, that she believe whatever Andrée told her, that she accept Andrée's picture of our harmonious relationship, our eager love-life, so that when I came to my senses I was unable to convince her that she need suffer no longer. And how could she know that I had changed, that I was no longer the person who had walked so lightly along the main street of Wellfleet, dressed in the cashmere turtleneck sweater Andrée had given me, borne on the air-cushion of my awakened senses, having been given a portion of Andrée's *joie de vivre*? During that time I had felt the energy of her happiness flow into me and saw her as subtle and infinitely refined.

> "*L'anémone et l'ancolie*
> *Ont poussé dans le jardin*
> *Où dort la mélancolie*
> *Entre l'amour et le dédain.*"

Over and over Andrée would murmur these lines of Apollinaire or quote endlessly in her musical voice: Racine, Verlaine, Baudelaire, and sing old French songs, bawdy and tender, while Marie-Claire and I listened, enchanted. Was it all pretense, her bubbling merriment, her love for the house, the Wellfleet life, even for the things we ate and drank, for which later she professed such scorn? Even then, though, she balked at the idea of eating a boiled egg as I did for breakfast every day, and sulked at the sight of the three identical eggcups I put on the breakfast table. They suggested equality between the three of us, a suggestion which had already become intolerable to her. She and I should have identical eggcups, she confided to me, and Marie-Claire a different kind. "*Je déteste le chiffre trois*," she had begun to say pointedly. "*Le chiffre trois*" was evidently inclusive of everyone except herself and me, for her face became stony if we questioned her about her husband or her children. My coming to my senses was a matter of registering these surprising transformations and feeling my tender image bruised by them, the loving cells gradually replaced by those that were dry, wary, and loveless.

Perhaps Andrée was suffering from her own surprises—at having discovered my puritan heart and all the limits that my scheduled habits imposed on me and everybody else. She had not expected the austerity of Wellfleet in November, with its cold winds and brooding sky, its limited coterie of friends, its non-existent amusements. We went to the Edmund Wilsons' for drinks ("she reminded me of one of Père Goriot's daughters," Edmund was later to say about Andrée), the first of several times when hard liquor had a disastrous effect on her. Perhaps something had been said at the Wilsons' to suggest that she, not Marie-Claire, was the third person in our triangle. In Canada later, the impulse to drink half a bottle of gin was triggered by the sight of a watercolor I had done of Marie-Claire, dressed in a yellow jacket and a green hat, with a winsome look on her slightly tilted face. In Canada she had let loose a diatribe against Marie-Claire with many intimate and gratuitous details which embarrassed the assembled guests, who knew nothing of our situation. I reacted with rage and sickness of soul, which I visited on Andrée as soon as she was lucid enough to listen to me. The hazard of living with her was that one never knew what would provoke her demons or how they would cause her to behave. In New York, she rushed into the path of an oncoming car and was jerked back just in time; in Brittany, she threw herself into a gorse bush and screamed; in Maine, she tried to leap out of the car. For a while these flurries of punishment, of herself and us, were balanced by the times when she bubbled with good spirits and worked her magic charms, when, reanimated by the return of the original Andrée, I, too, would feel an inebriating *joie de vivre*.

A chemical change was at work in me in the interval between Andrée's two visits to Wellfleet, and I remember clearly the day of her second arrival at the Boston airport, this time with Marie-

Claire, when she appeared to me as a stranger. I saw a small, almost dumpy woman, her legs clad in thick black tights, a short black cape over her shoulders, her head like a crystal egg set on her short neck. Her face with its highbridged nose (like the Ram of her zodiacal sign) was an angry red and wore an impatient and disdainful look. I caught this look and the flouncing movement of her shoulders before she saw me; she looked spoiled and worldly. Who was this person? Did I have some kind of a relationship with her? I felt dismay at the thought that between her visits I had told her over and over again in letters that I loved her, though it was not this person but that other one I first saw, who had such a vulnerable and sensitive face and such a happy child's smile. But now I must pretend to be glad to see the new Andrée, for there was Marie-Claire, who seemed to love the new Andrée as much as the old one, anxious, tender, hovering over her friend, who in response shook back her silver hair with an irritable jerk. I knew this gesture, even liked it, for it had reminded me of an impatient tomboy in those first uncritical days. And now it had become as sharp and menacing as the cocking of a trigger. Seeing me, she launched into an account of the horrors of the trip: the baby crying in the seat behind her, the horrible fellow passengers, the long wait at customs, but was something the matter with me? For she had absorbed my coolness and was suddenly concerned and subservient. We climbed into the Jeep and she pushed close to my side, turning her back on Marie-Claire and her head toward me with an adoring gaze that seemed to bore through my right ear into my skull. Her bag was packed with presents for me, which she pulled out like a magician when we reached the house. I received these presents from Dior and St. Laurent, which Marie-Claire in her generous folly had helped to pay for, with joy and dread, the ominous feeling that they bound me as tightly to Andrée as a pair of handcuffs. They held the import of a potlatch; I was meant in the next round to outdo their munificence.

Somewhere among the ancient treasures of France there is a stone sculpture of a pageboy dressed in a coat of mail, with his hands clasped on a sword planted in front of him, a portrait of

Andrée as she saw herself and as I first saw her, standing on sturdy legs, in readiness to serve her knight. I did not want to be her knight, since an ideal relationship for me is that between two knight-comrades, but I was flattered for a time by her uncritical adoration, little knowing that I would later think of it as merely another of the roles she played so convincingly. Inside her page's clothes was a milky-pale woman's body with heavy hips and small breasts, and a seeming absence of muscles, particularly in her arms and hands. The latter had little fingers like limp and boneless appendages which had lost their usefulness, curved, isolated from the others, rejected. They had a certain eloquence, those helpless little fingers, a menace, reminding me that strength lies not in appearances but in what is hidden, or in the sum of the parts. Andrée's legs could carry her up mountains and along beaches with amazing speed, and her delicate white hands and arms were as strong as the mad Mrs. Rochester's. She had a compact body like a porpoise's; she swam great distances and might have lived in the sea in another life, for her hands and feet were like flippers untouched by evolution. She loved to take baths and would fill up the tub to the brim every day and immerse herself for an hour or so, and appeared afterwards as fresh as a newly-bathed baby, in a white judo tunic, walking into the living room with a swift, gliding movement of her little feet as if she were swimming in the ocean depths.

Love persuades two people that they think alike, and the death of love kills this illusion. Thoughts no longer mesh together with the sensuality of bodies meshing; instead comes something like a physical blow or the sudden clashing of horns. Andrée and I, Aries and Taurus, our horns locked in the meeting of stubborn heads. Perhaps she felt that I could be trained to agree with her as she was training me in matters of taste; my pliability in some matters hid my intransigence in others. As love drains away, the self takes shape again, takes extreme forms of opposition as a way of fending off the other. Andrée and I began to dislike what each revered and to have those fruitless discussions born of the need to disagree, adored by many men and by all French people, who feel it a duty to temper the enthusiasm of intemperate Anglo-Saxons. The art of French conversation consists not of saying what you believe but of hiding what you believe by tangling your opponent in a shining web of contradiction. Andrée was irritated by my solemn determination to get somewhere in conversations and by my respect for museums, cathedrals and music. When we went to hear the Gregorian service at Solesmes, she said, "*Je trouve ça très beau et très ennuyeux.*" To be bored by something beautiful was never to lose sight of one's right to put down the mighty by an act of critical possession. Andrée knew the proper tone of indifference to take in talking about great art, or, if it was *her* subject, the proper tone of reverence. Gradually I began to realize that she found my labored opinions boring, and that her contradictory reactions to them were a way of overcoming her boredom. For a time I was putty in her hands, glad to have my French corrected and my knowledge of poetry enlarged, liking my education in food and clothes and exquisite objects, but here, too, our natures fatally clashed, my puritanism running into her worldliness. The ideal of French perfection extends from head to feet and any lapse is instantly visible to searching French eyes. Andrée not only wore clothes from St. Laurent, Givenchy and Dior, but also had her hair cut by the best coiffeur in Paris; her nails were manicured, and in summer every toenail wore its blood-red mask, which like semaphore signals drew attention to the elegance of her sandals. The hair I washed and cut myself, my naked toenails, and the big men's sandals I wore, undid the effect of my St. Laurent sweater and were only excusable because I was an American in whom sins of taste could be understood if not forgiven. I remember the real pain Andrée felt at the sight of my toenails, those immodest reminders that a foot is a foot and not an object to be adorned.

These things would be too insignificant to talk about except in the context of Fashion, a god who is more tyrannical than Jehovah, worshipped by millions of human beings of both sexes, who decrees that I will feel uneasy if my pants do not conform to this year's decree, who decides that my state of well-being will be enhanced if I wear an Hermès coat, and that I will skulk down a Paris street like a pariah if I feel that my clothes are being tried and found wanting. This is ridiculous, I struggle against it, I exercise the liberty of my hands and feet—my home-cut hair, my flat-heeled shoes, and the impertinent pallor of my toenails. Fashion should be the least important concern of women's lives and yet they are enslaved by it. In its name, barbarous cruelties have been committed, bodies have been mutilated, constrained and almost suffocated, animals have been tortured, women have allowed their freedom to move to be inhibited, and inordinate demands to be made on their time. The exigence of fashion answers a deep need in people to move in unison like minnows or starlings, above all, to pass. How many people are not frightened by the thought of announcing an unacceptable difference from others. The Nazis required that cloth emblems be worn—yellow stars by Jews, pink triangles by homosexuals, a diabolical design to legitimize prejudice by making the hidden difference visible. Could this explain my exaggerated misery when I was looked up and down by the French sitting in sidewalk cafés, that I could feel the pink triangle blossoming on my chest? Expensive clothes drew looks to themselves, I noticed, but looks which obliterated the pink triangle; they contained the magic which enabled me to pass.

I have been thinking about how the idea of passing is born of every form of racism, for the victim of racism instinctively adopts the protective coloring that will allow him/her to pass, to live invisibly with the enemy. These adaptations follow a law of self-preservation, just as insects have learned to look like leaves, sticks or other more threatening insects, anything rather than their vulnerable selves; they have adopted a camouflage to say, "Do not mistake us for prey." Human beings, in using similar defenses, incorporate the racism that has victimized them; homosexuals who do not "look" homosexual sometimes profess hate for "butch" women or effeminate men, Jews who have passed are sometimes anti-semitic, black people in many places judge their own social status by the relative paleness or darkness of their skin. This is the worst aspect of passing—that you become what you imitate, and that disdain for your own kind, the member of your own kind who is too conspicuous or too courageous to try to pass, enters into your heart and you become a traitor, denying like Peter when the moment comes to declare your real allegiance, or keeping silent. Silence, which you call discretion or the right to privacy, allows you to have it both ways, to be at home in either camp, but more often the person who has succeeded in passing is doubly afraid, afraid of the wrath of both sides, and keeps her secret with a special dread of its being discovered. The lesbians of my generation had and still have tricks of adaptation, strange disguises which do not disguise but are *accepted* as disguises. A whole symbolic language of disguise, almost surrealist, like Magritte's visual puns (shoe equals key, etc.). Our puns were social and patriarchal: skirt equals heterosexual, silence equals "innocence." Not so long ago we played this game so well that we felt comfortable playing it and grew into our disguises, almost as though the puns had been invented with our consent. Like mice that have been brought up with cats and are not eaten. First we enjoyed the luxury of not being eaten; then we became cats ourselves and were stricken with terror at the idea that we would be taken for mice, that the mouse in us *showed*. In extreme cases, some of us became more ferocious toward mice than cats in order to show that there was no mouse in us. The less extreme simply adapted so perfectly, felt so comfortable that they saw (or see) no reason for changing. As cats they were never persecuted. I have heard lesbian friends say, "No one has ever made me feel unhappy about being a lesbian." We oldtime lesbians occupied a very strange position, thanks to our non-passing which was accepted as passing, we were able to infiltrate the patriarchy and become an honored part of it. We gratefully accepted our position in society as honorary cats and took our nourishment from the masters of literature, painting, and music—all men; the art of becoming an honorary cat was to mimic a cat's behavior and to eat catfood. Hence the anomaly of the closeted lesbian artist who refuses both the lesbian label and that of the "woman artist," for she has passed into the heaven of universality, which really means acceptance in a man's world. I still sometimes feel the old agreeable complicity with men, by means of which all differences seem to fall away. As an artist my creative cells were formed from deep draughts from the patriarchal dish, which nourished body, soul, and mind, and I still live with these ideas and ways of speaking, painting, writing, which I have taken in and give out automatically. A feminist problem lies just here, I think, in the absorption by women of men's thought, so that they give it out as well as men, with a justifiable pride — philosophy, poetry, psychology — without turning it to their own uses. Can we turn it to our own uses? I think so if we acknowledge that merely to imitate it is a form of passing.

Newborn infants are immediately taught to pass as boys or girls; the whole of life is an effort to pass in one way or another, and the social fabric holds together because of a kind of invisible intimidation that persuades people that they will be outcasts from society if they do not follow its rules. Fashion has made possible an everyday kind of passing, born of the need to look "properly" dressed, to propitiate some of the false gods. If you see a lesbian dressed in tattered jeans and an old workshirt, you can be sure she is no longer in the closet, that she has stopped propitiating the gods, and is now expressing her right to feel comfortable and her pride in being recognized. And those of us who are still manipulated by the false god of fashion — do we do any harm? Don't we participate, through our consent, in one of the dubious communions of racism?

Yesterday, I saw a friend wearing a pink triangle and I thought, would I have the courage to do that? And if I don't want to wear one, isn't it because I am still hoping to deflect immediate recognition and judgment? If homosexuals were required to wear pink triangles, would I wear one before I was forced to? If Jews were required to wear yellow stars, would I declare my solidarity by wearing a yellow star? I hope so. I think I would, sitting here comfortably in my safety zone. But how can we predict what we will do in extreme states of terror or pain, whom we will betray, into which haven of racism we will creep despite all our good intentions? Aren't many attempts to pass born of intolerable fear? There in the little pink plastic triangle my friend was wearing lay the limits of my own courage, sign of a small betrayal, yet I realize with relief that I no longer care if I'm recognized and that I've almost ceased to hide. Only the other day, Delfina, the Italian woman who comes to clean for me, demonstrated as much anxiety about my feet as Andrée had. "You should wear higher heels," she said. She scrutinizes my clothes with a hawk's eye. "You're very elegant today," she says on occasion, meaning with the exception of my flat heels. Lapses form the norm of the acceptable woman, one who by her shoes or the ways she wears her hair, poses no uncomfortable, unanswerable questions, working their way like splinters into the mind of a Delfina, who, like a host of women, with her sharp eye for convention, examines a photograph of friends at a party. "They're all women," she says. The pink triangle seems to come dimly to life, like something seen under water, for Delfina's knowledge of this special world outside her own is necessarily limited. All she knows is that according to her lights something is wrong.

Virginia Woolf used to feel that people were laughing at the way she dressed; to walk down a street made her miserable. Sometimes, indeed, they *were* laughing at her, with the heartlessness of chickens closing in on a strange hen. These reactions are rooted in our animal nature, it seems, enforced by convention and snobbery, dignified by taboos, by dress codes, and in the thousand little ways human beings invent to form their eternal hierarchies. I remember that when I was in the WAVES, when the clothes-anxiety was dispelled by the wearing of a uniform—even then the uniform permitted degrees of perfection. There were silver-plated bars for a lieutenant and those made of solid silver, which glowed, we thought, with a special light; there was a hand-embroidered eagle with gold and silver thread to put on your hat, or the regulation kind, immediately recognizable, and you could have your uniform made of expensive material and specially tailored, with the result that our uniform, which already denoted our difference from enlisted women, began to show evidence of the same rivalry which is peculiar to civilian life.

Andrée did not recognize the choosing of expensive clothes as snobbery but dignified her choice as an art and an exercise of the senses, for touching fine cashmere or tweed gave her as much pleasure as looking at a perfectly-cut coat. And my Achilles heel was my fear of being found wanting in this fine aesthetic sense which seemed to include every aspect of life. Andrée confused me sometimes by falling in love with some humble and tattered garment that I had worn for fifteen years, by literally taking it off my back and putting it on her own, or by persuading me to look for something exactly like it. It now seems to me that this was less a tribute to my taste than a desire to possess something of my essence, for she believed in this sort of magic rite. Maybe the exchange of clothes would bring us closer together? She was angry and disbelieving when I wanted my coat back; the magic had failed, and its failure could only mean that I was taking myself back along with the coat.

The snobbery of Andrée and Antoine was like a many-armed Shiva, reaching out in every direction, embracing almost the entire world: the poor, the uneducated, the bourgeoisie, all Jews, all people of whatever color, all radicals, feminists and self-proclaimed lesbians; it was a snobbery almost charitable in the magnitude of its scope, an anti-charity, like anti-Christ, for the effect of their disdain was to make one wish to defend all those they despised and to dislike the small circle of their elect. The net of their snobbery had meshes so fine that if you escaped by being "well-born" or having money, you could be caught because you liked some writer on their index or because of the shoes you wore. Snobbery comes from having mastered the art of passing not because of fear but because of its rewards, pride of passage into an arbitrary heaven, and a feeling of superiority to all those who are unable to do the same. It has the same root as racism, each feeds the other, each uses the same arguments to justify its existence. The pleasure of passing, when the passer's disguise is so perfect that there is no longer a danger, sometimes outweighs its pain. To outwit the enemy by playing his game, to keep him from knowing one's secret; the turning of a sense of oppression into a game or an art is to dull its edges. Antoine and Andrée had no sense of oppression; they swam in their racism like fish in the sea. And just as Andrée would not have acknowledged that she was snobbish or racist, would have thought up fifty reasons why she was neither, she would not have acknowledged that there were parts of herself in hiding, that everybody who has passed has a hidden self, a denied self, the one that is vulnerable to the racism and snobbery one has assimilated.

BARBARA DEMING

A BOOK OF TRAVAIL—AND OF A
HUMMING UNDER MY FEET*

In 1950-51, Deming, young then, but already in full possession of her writer's craft and consciousness, went for the first time to Europe and lived and traveled there for more than a year. Italy, France, Germany, Greece, Spain—traveling usually third class, with a knapsack and her father's quilt, she took her writer's notes and kept letters, etc. Soon after, conceiving the whole experience as central in her life, and as passionately unified by her falling in love during this period, she set out to write of it—and finished a first chapter. But she couldn't continue. Friends discouraged her—because she was writing about a lesbian and this was not only taboo then, it was not considered an authentic hold upon reality.

Times change. Having a good memory, having kept the notes, letters, etc., she is able to give us now this experience, to resee it through her powers of a writer who is also a poet. Since the writing was postponed twenty years, we get the benefit of Deming's later perspective on this material—showing us a young woman in the process of her radicalizing, before she is aware of theory. The portion here is a good example of this. And of the religious or epic quality of this work, a woman's epic for our age of awareness.
—Jane Gapen

[At this point in the narrative, Barbara is in Greece. She has tried to persuade Carlotta, with whom she's in love, to join her; but Carlotta has written that she can't. She's added that if Barbara feels like returning to Italy, they can say goodbye there before Carlotta leaves for the U.S.—to get married. In the scene before

---

*From Chapter 15.

*this, Barbara has watched a gypsy whose wife was about to take
ship dance a long goodbye. Small cuts in the text are indicated by
ellipses. Ed.]*

"So goodbye"—yes, strange words. But I decided of course to
return to Italy to say them. To dance them in my own way, if I
could find the spirit. Could I find it?

I had had an experience on the boat returning from Crete that
had confused and *dispirited me.* I'd spent some time with the
gypsy mother and daughter—conversing in gestures, sharing the
food we'd brought along. But toward the end of the day two Greek
soldiers who were fluent in English struck up a conversation.
They then taught me the words of some of the Greek songs I particularly loved. First sang them—their voices raised above the
complaining voices of a goat and two lambs tethered on the deck
nearby. Then wrote the words down in my notebook for me. After
night had fallen I said goodnight to them and to my gypsy friends
and wrapped myself in my quilt in a sort of hatchway that looked
like a good spot—just under the captain's deck. It was a chilly
night; one of the soldiers came over soon and asked could he
share one corner of the quilt. It was such a large quilt, he
pleaded. I told him no. And he lay down nearby. And then began
to sigh to himself and to mutter, like a peevish child. Most of the
other passengers had brought some kind of covering. I could see
the gypsy mother and child across the way wrapped together in a
bright blanket cocoon. His friend had a sweater, but he hadn't, he
muttered. "Listen to my teeth chattering," he said. The quilt *was*
a very large one. And both of us of course were fully dressed. I
had my coat on. I decided suddenly that it wasn't really fair that
he should shiver. I lifted a corner of the quilt, moved to the far
side of it and said: "here." He quickly moved in under.

I heard a cackle of laughter from the captain's deck above. And
a few shouted words. And then a second man's laughter.

"What is he saying?" I asked.

"He says if he sees any funny business below he'll toss a

bucket on water on us," said the soldier.

"He won't see any funny business," I said.

I began to doze off. The waves hissed against the side of the ship. The goat and the two lambs continued to complain. And then I felt a stealthy motion as the soldier moved just a little closer—I felt his hand very quietly placed on my thigh. As I sat up and pulled the quilt off him and wrapped it round myself and told him he'd better leave. And he left. I heard ribald laughter again from above.

The gypsy child woke me at dawn, and the mother suggested—in sign language—that we have some coffee. We stood in line for it together at the ship's kitchen; drank it quietly, seated on her blanket. Then as I was leaving the boat, the soldier reappeared, stepped close to my side and suggested that we find a hotel room—where there'd be no ship's captain watching from above. And I had to explain that my letting him under the quilt really had been because his teeth had been chattering.

"Then you don't like men?" he asked me with an almost sneer.

I believed in love, I told him. I added that I was sorry if he'd misunderstood me.

He gave a contemptuous shrug and strode off.

I'm sorry to report that I left the ship in a state of shame. It's hard to admit to this now. In what a criss-cross of bonds I allowed myself to be caught. I would have been ashamed if I'd continued to refuse a corner of my quilt to him; so how could I be ashamed, too, that I had offered it? But I was. I would have been ashamed if I had accepted his advances; so how could I be ashamed, too, that I had refused them? But I was. And ashamed—not for him but for myself—that he had made them. Ashamed to be a woman is what it amounted to. "Unfair!" I can cry now—"Unfair that women are expected always to feel ashamed that we are sexual beings whatever our behavior!" But I didn't know how to cry this then.

I think back to my earliest experience of my sexuality. I'll not count a few tentative childhood inquiries made of my body, of other child bodies. I am sixteen. In love with an older woman—Zoe. I begin to spill over with poems. Which I give to her. Poems which speak my love. One day I ask her, "May I kiss you?" She tells me, "Yes." I give her a childish kiss. "That's not the way to kiss," she whispers. And then she shows me how to kiss. I drink sweetness. On a day soon after, we are lying alone in her garden. The sun high. The grass in which we lie warm. I have flung my arm around her, to draw her close to me — wishing for more kisses. In a languorous motion I can recall still she moves a thigh between my thighs. And magic travels across my body — wakes me now as if from long sleep. I give a small cry of surprise. She smiles at this. Her smile is summer. And shame does not exist. It is not shame that wakes in me with this wakening of sexuality, but my first vivid sense that I may be able to find a life that I want; that there are deeps in me from which I can draw. And poems, poems. Shame has still to be learned. Shame — that steals us from ourselves.

But I had learned it by the time I write of. And now when I thought ahead to seeing you again, in Rome, it was hard to imagine myself at ease with you, in equilibrium. The cackling laughter of the captain was in my ears.

By the calendar you'd drawn I had about two weeks left to spend in Greece before catching a boat to Italy. I . . . traveled down through the Peloponnesus — to see Olympia, Epidauros, Mycenae.

The country round Olympia was lusher, less shorn of trees than the country I had seen until then. At the temple site, the many stone columns stood among living columns of tall pines. The smell of resin was in the air. And the shrill of insects. I wandered through the ruins, and then through the wooded hills behind them. Returned and sat among the gray pillars and wrote to you and to my family. Sat on past nightfall. An owl began to call with husky voice from high in the tree under which I sat. Called and called. I listened to it thirstily. Owl, call me back to myself. I watched the stars come out in their many delicate colors. Or rather, as my journal notes, I tried to but I never quite succeeded in seeing a new star appear — I could merely notice, of one after another: Now it is there. But as, one after another, they surprised me, the captain's hateful laughter faded from my mind.

I woke the next morning at 5:00 to catch my bus south, and so made the long ride through mountain country sleepily—though the jolting of the bus did wake me repeatedly from napping. At Argos I changed to another rackety bus which took me to Napflion. And at Napflion I changed to another rackety bus which took me to Ligorio. There I checked my knapsack at the small hotel and decided not to wait for a ride to Epidauros but to start out walking.

It was a sparkling day and I began to wake fully. I had walked a mile or so when I saw a tiny figure ahead on the road. When I came up, I found that it was a little girl waiting there—clasping a bouquet of poppies and delicate delphiniums. She held it out to me with an eager gesture. And spoke—as a question—the beautiful Greek word for flowers: "Looloothia?" I can hear again the sweet high lilt of her voice singing the word. She drew out the accent on the second "loo"—"Loolooooothia?" I took the flowers in my hands. Was she selling them or giving them? I had to ask myself—as I had asked when I'd met the girl on the path in Taormina. Both, I decided again. So I thanked her first. And then gave her a good-sized bill. She opened her eyes wide. And ran off lickety-split to a friend I noticed now, another girl, who waited for her under a distant tree. I walked on, feeling blessed by that meeting, but also wishing again with a pang that I had had something better than money to give. How could money equal poppies and delphiniums?

After another mile, a bus came along and I hailed it and hopped on. It was carrying a group of students and their teacher-guide to the ancient outdoor theater. It was easy to keep a distance from them, once at the site, for they stayed together. I climbed way up to the highest row of stone step-seats—where the air was full of bird calls—and stared about me. Remembered the plays I had read that had once been staged here under the sky, the stories of Orestes and Electra, Oedipus, Antigone. I found soon that I was sitting there awed, the drama of my own life overshadowed by these classic dramas—of faith kept with royal fathers. faith kept with royal brothers. I didn't say it consciously to myself, yet sat there knowing that what seemed in my own life of the very deepest moment would not have found celebration here.

I started to roam about. The group of students began climbing up to the top and so I moved down and to another side of the immense theatre. Then they moved down the steps again, they got into the waiting bus and went off; but I had decided to stay on. The birds called with sweet voices—across the bowl of the theater and across the neighboring fields. I began to wander through the fields.

There was a jumble of fallen temple stones here, scattered wide, lying pale in the fading light. A few horses were browsing, and I passed a tiny goat halfway up a tree, nibbling leaves. Overhead the evening clouds moved rapidly. I experienced now as I walked about the sharpest kind of loneliness. I remembered the soldier's contemptuous shrug; I remembered . . . the words you spoke to me on the street in Rome: "When a woman comes too close to me, I resent it." I remembered Nell's leaving me to marry my brother. Had I courage to be the sexual self that I was? To act out truthfully this part for which, it seemed, no play was written?

Then staring at the lightly tossing many-colored grasses at my feet, I remembered suddenly Elevsis and could amost hear again that curious humming in my inner ear, feel that vibration in my limbs. "My answer is yes," I said to myself—without words. I roamed into a farther field. The scattered marble fragments were fewer here. Near the field's corner, among the grasses, I saw a gleaming stone and moved toward it. It was a fragment of a fallen statue—a woman's torso, without head or arms, and leaning slightly. I sat down on another fallen bit of marble and gazed at it. The stone breasts shone among the tossing grasses. "Yes I am, I am this sexual self," I said. And stood up, trembling, and went over and knelt and put my hands against the shining ancient breasts. And said: "I am this self that I am. I affirm it." I sang to myself: Yes I am. And I will not be robbed of my sex. And I will not be shamed." The stone breasts were cool under my hands, with the coolness of water found at a spring, life-giving. I felt the spirit of the stone enter my hands with this coolness and enter my soul. I sang (without any sound): "Yes. It is the truth about me and so I will live it."

It felt to me, I can remember, like a very bold action to be taking. Even though no one watched—except for browsing animals. As I rose from where I had been sitting and took those few steps and knelt. It felt as though I were taking my very life in my hands when I pressed them against those cool breasts. I remember the crickets singing round me. I remember trembling. The trembling was like a life current that was shaking me. I knelt there a long time . . .

My story moves toward this moment and past it, moves away from it and back to it again.

I wandered off toward the road, turning often to look back at that image in the grass. As I look back now. Someone was calling to the horses—with a melodious almost teasing whistle. They lifted their heads, then lowered them and ate a little more grass, then—as the whistling persisted—decided to trot off. After I'd walked a little way down the road a man on a motorcycle with sidecar drove along and I hailed him and asked for a ride into Ligorio, for it was turning dark now. I had to squat on the edge of the sidecar, which was full of cans. And at the little hotel where I'd left my knapsack I found that all the rooms had been taken. The man at the desk and I had not understood each other earlier. But as always one English-speaking Greek soon appeared—a gnarled man who told me that he and his wife had a spare room and put up paying guests. They would feed me, too. So I followed him home.

. . . The guest room was a large room with two beds and a number of honored mementoes very carefully placed. He pointed out a lute he used to play, hung under a portrait of himself and his wife . . . He turned to me and puckered his lips: "A kiss?" I shook my head. He looked surprised and sad but didn't try to insist . . .

In the morning I decided to start off walking toward Mycenae, and again to hail the bus when it happened to come along. He walked along with me for a while, for he had work to do in one of his several fields. He had wheat fields, he told me, a hundred olive trees, and grapes. Before he turned off the road he gave me, for my trip, a large hunk of bread and two onions. I thanked him and put out my hand, which he quickly raised to his lips. And then, before I could stop him, he kissed the inside of my arm, too. As I moved off, he called after me, "I'll dream of you, my daughter. If I were not so old, I'd not let you go."

I'd walked a mile or so—passing workers in the fields—when I saw three women and two small children resting in a field under a tree. They waved and beckoned: "Ella!"—Come! So I joined them under the tree. They offered me wine (tossing out what was left in the cup—with a splendid gesture—before re-filling it and passing it to me), they offered me bread and olives and a dish of scrambled eggs in oil. They knew no English but were so very eager to hear who I was and why I was on the road that with the help of my dictionary we did talk a bit. When either they or I became confused about just what was being said— which was often—we'd begin to laugh. We spent much of the time laughing like this—the children laughing too. There would be a festival in the fields outside a nearby chapel, the very next day, they told me. Why didn't I stay and take part in it? The youngest of the women—the merriest laugher, very skinny, her head wrapped in a sweat-stained white cloth—told me I could stay the night at her house. I thought for a moment of saying yes. But first I should go to see the ruins at Mycenae, I told them—for I had just so much time—but I'd return in the morning for the festival. They rose to go back to work now.

The day before, on the bus to Ligorio, I'd sat next a young school teacher who spoke some English and she had invited me to stop off and visit the two-room schoolhouse where she taught. I'd promised to visit her today. After a few miles walk I reached the town she'd named and when I spoke the word for "school" a boy who for some mysterious reason was not attending school that day gestured for me to follow him and guided me to the right building—on a back street, near a rapid little river. On the banks of the river a group of women were on their knees slap-slapping their laundry against the wet rocks. I could still hear this sound every now and then from inside the school building. The teacher—Katerina—was surprised but very pleased to see me. She introduced me to the children and then continued for a while to teach the class. The children were doing sums—writing them on the blackboard and then chanting the answers. Their mouths in wonderful grimaces. Their chanting rather like the chanting I'd heard in the churches.

Katerina soon left the room to bring the other teacher in to meet me—a curlyheaded man with yellow shoes who I learned later was her fiancé. She referred to him as "Sir." "Sir says . . ." They took me into his room, too, to meet his class. I still remember the problem he had written on the blackboard for them to solve. Katerina translated it for me. (Sir spoke no English.) "A man has 142 children. A wolf eats 30. How many are left?"

At lunch time the children ran off to their homes and Katerina asked me and Sir to have lunch with her at her place—which was a room one reached by some outside steps in a house next the village church. In the room were a large iron double bed with one blanket, a seachest (stamped US), a small marbletop table and two chairs, a few clothes hung on a hook on the wall and a small suitcase. I asked for the bathroom and she led me downstairs again and, with visible embarrassment, to the stable attached to the house. She peered at me as if to ask: "Does this upset you?" And when I smiled at her to let her know that it didn't upset me in the least, she smiled back, surprised and relieved. Then she waited for me at the head of the stairs with a pitcher of water, a towel, and a new cake of Hermes soap. And we all three washed our hands. Back in the room she put the soap away very carefully. She'd put a clean striped cloth on the little table and now served us batter cakes—cooked in the kitchen she shared with others; cheese and olives and retsina. As there were only two chairs, she sat on the bed.

She, too, was full of questions about my travels. When she looked at me I could see that she was trying to imagine her own self wandering like this through a wider world than Ligorio. She carefully translated everything that I said for her fiancé. At one point he made the suggestion I'd become used to by now—that *I* marry him and take him back with me to the USA. And she carefully translated this, too, though coloring a bit as she did so.

I told her I was headed this day for Mycenae and she said that the next bus left at 4:00. But couldn't I stay over and take a bus the next day? I would be back this way the next day, I told her— for I'd be going to the festival I'd heard about. I tried out my Greek and explained now "*agapo choros*"—meaning to say "I love dancing." But perhaps I pronounced the words strangely. A happy blush spread over her face. "Thank you," she said, "I love you more."

And now it was time for school again. As we passed the river I saw her glance at its darting waters and for just a moment her eyes held a look of such longing to be able to dart across new distances too that I stared at her. But in the next moment that look was veiled. Sir asked her some question and she turned to him with sweet gravity.

She had the children sing for me that afternoon. And just before I left, she asked one little girl to go out and pick me some flowers. The girl returned with a few hollyhock heads—just the heads. She asked another girl to go and bring back roses—and that girl returned with a few nipped-off roses' heads. Then Katerina asked one of the older boys to guide me to the right place to hail the bus. In parting, she held my hands for a minute. Katerina, I have often thought of you.

Mycenae wasn't many miles from Ligorio. But I had to change buses along the way and there was a long wait for the second bus. So by the time I'd been dropped off at a crossroads near Mycenae it was much later than I'd expected it to be. The sun was low in the sky. And I'd expected the ruins to be close to the hotel where Katerina had told me I'd find a room. But when I'd walked there I found that the ruins were still a mile or so away— up in the hills behind this little town. I'd asked two little boys the way to the hotel—La Belle Hèlêne—and they'd walked me there. I'd taken a room, left my knapsack at the desk, hurried out again and started off along the rutted road up into the hills — and heard a small sound and turned and saw that the boys were following me now at a distance. So I gestured to them and they came running up. I'd learned that the only bus that could get me back in time for the festival the next day left early in the morning, so my one chance to explore the ruins was now. But night was closing in. The man at the desk in fact had advised me that I'd not be able to see anything by the time I reached the site. I figured if I walked fast enough I might prove him wrong; but I was happy to have my guides.

The road wound up and round steeply to the left. My notes recall "strange gray forbidding wondrous hills" surrounding us soon. We passed a shepherd and his flock on a slope above us and the shepherd's dog came rushing down at us, snarling. One of the boys gave it a kick at which the shepherd came rushing down, waving a large stick. Was this to chastise the dog or to chastise the boy? We didn't wait to learn but dashed forward, up the road. And into the dark. For the sun had by now dropped behind the hills.

When we slowed our steps again, I noticed the lights from fires shepherds had built twinkling in the distance from various hills. The older boy took my hand and led me off the road to the left — into the hillside itself it seemed for a strange moment. "*Tholos,*" he said — "Agamemnon." It was the first of the great "beehive" tombs. I peered up and could dimly see the great stone lintel of its gateway high above our heads. Once inside I could see nothing. But the boy led me to the curved far wall and placed my hands against its stones. Then they both did a fierce dance, stamping their heels hard against the ground, and the echoes of their steps, rebounding from the walls, made the shape and size of the place known to me. I joined in the dance myself.

When we had climbed the road to the top of the hill, we came to the Gate of Lions — set in ramparts built of huge stones, the walls tunneled in toward the gate, its great lintel again high above our heads. Above this lintel two stone lionesses—lacking heads—reared up on their hindlegs, with forefeet set upon a kind of altar. A sliver of moon was in the sky and I could just make out their sinewy presences. Squinting up at them, I remembered for a moment the dream in which I wrestled with an animal quite like one of these. The older boy again took me by the hand and we passed through the gate. And now he led me up a kind of ramp to the left—the younger boy giggling a little. Then pointed down into mysterious hollows. Led me—slow-motion so that I shouldn't stumble—down and up various steps. And sometimes over low walls. And to a lookout spot—where we could stare down at the faintly discernible plain of Argos and across to distant lights at the verge of the darkened sea. It could have been from here that Clytemnestra had watched for Agamemnon's ship to return from the war against Troy. And it was somewhere within these walls that she had killed him. And it was somewhere within these walls that she herself had been killed.

The boy led me down and around through the almost-dark, where he placed my hand on an earthenware pipe—and spoke the word for water. This was a secret cistern, I would read later, disguised as a tomb—so those under siege in this citadel could always find water.

Then he led me up again and around and under some scaffolding into another great tomb, but this one no longer intact but open to the stars. And he spoke the name of Clytemnestra. The husband-killer. In the distance I could hear shepherds pipes now. Teasing sounds—trembling on the air as thoughts can tremble in the mind without one's knowing that one is thinking them. I didn't at all at that time know what all my thoughts about Clytemnestra were. The plays that I had read named her killing of Agamemnon a crime. But his killing of one of their daughters—as a sacrifice to bring fair winds so that he needn't wait to sail off to war—this was justified. And the killing of Clytemnestra by her son, to avenge his father—this was justified too. By the "gods." The mother's anger alone remained unjustified—even her two surving daughters wanting her dead. It would be almost twenty years before I would dare to admit to myself that I felt threatened by this judgment of who had a right to anger and who had not. (It was not until I read Kate Millett's words about the ancient story in *Sexual Politics* that I admitted it—with a bursting out from within me then of all my rebel feelings.) At the time I knew only that to think of Clytemnestra was painful, and I was glad that I was exploring this site under cover of night.

Cover of night. Years later now, I muse about my own mother's anger against her husband, my father. About the fact that it was under cover of night that she spoke to me of its cause. And the fact, too, that she never did actually name her anger anger.

I remember her first confiding in me. I am sixteen. I am in love with Zoe. I have been lying in bed unable to sleep—so brimming with this love, which wants to spill over, wants to speak. I decide to tell my mother my feelings. For the only in any way comparable feelings I have ever experienced have been feelings for *her*. I tiptoe into her room. "Are you awake still?" I ask her. She is awake by now. I whisper to her, "I am in love, I am in love!" She listens, tender and unjudging. I am shivering. She makes room for me next to her in bed. I smell the sweet slightly milky smell of her. Which calms me—as it used to calm me when I was a child. Her long lank hair lies next to me on the pillow. And the dark lies next to us.

And she begins to tell me of a time when *she* was utterly in love. Not with my father. She had never been in love with my father—only fond of him. Her mother had persuaded her to enter this marriage—assuring her that love would follow marriage. But it was love for another man that had followed. Some years later—after three of her children had been born. Then she had asked my father for a divorce. But he had refused. Arguing that marriage vows should not be broken. Sure of his correctness in this. When she had insisted, he had presented her with the most painful of choices: stay in the marriage and never see the other man again, or join the other man and lose her children. He would ask his sister to help him raise us, he told her. My mother had chosen not to lose her children.

I think back and can remember in her telling of this story no anger directly expressed. She expressed only her sense of loss: she could smell still the stale cigarette smoke in the telephone booth from which she called her lover—to tell him she could never see him again. I remember my own anger—and dismay—that my father, honorable in so very many ways, had felt it right to hold her captive, felt it right to claim sole authority to say what would become of *us*. But I could make out no anger in my mother's voice—strangely light—almost singsong—as if she were speaking of all this from a distance, safe distance. From cover.

Cover of night. It is some years later. My mother and I are making a long nighttime drive together, after a family visit. Sharing the driving. Our eyes fixed on the highway before us, a narrow tunnel through the dark. We have been talking about a young couple we know whose marriage has just broken apart—though everyone had assumed the two were happy. I ask my mother, "When you were first married, before you'd fallen in love, really in love with that other man—did you ever *think* that you were in love with Dad?" She is silent. Shrugs. And then in a dull voice she begins to tell me: "Every night at bedtime I would simply go upstairs with him, I would perform my wifely duty. Every night—" And again I can make out no anger. She speaks almost as a medium would speak in a trance. I listen in pain and wonder. Eyes fixed on the highway.

And then I ask her: "When Dad refused to let you leave him—when he told you he could take your children from you—weren't you terribly angry? Didn't you want some kind of revenge?"

"Revenge?" she asks, startled.

I say quickly, "I wouldn't blame you at all if you had wanted it. Perhaps to turn our affections from him if you could?" (I think she *has* wanted this.)

She says woodenly, "He thought he was right."

"Oh, I know," I say, "I know."

As we hug goodnight, that night, at the end of the drive, I feel very close to her, and touched that she has been willing to speak to me as intimately as she has. But in the morning, to my dismay, she stammers out, "That drive last night — I feel as though it were a bad dream I had dreamed. Trapped in the car, driving through a bad dream."

I am sorry, Mother.

I named your anger. A woman's anger is not supposed to be named. A woman's anger is supposed to be cause for shame.

Another memory rises in me. I am sixteen or seventeen. One day Zoe tells me that she's insisted to my mother that she (my mother) mustn't ever feel she has to sleep with my father when she doesn't want to. Tonguetied at her words — and all that they bring to mind — I inwardly fiercely assent. Fiercely assent, and yet and yet — one evening not long after, passing the open doorway of my mother's room, I see my father sitting there on the edge of her bed, waiting for her. In the raggedy old bathrobe that he has worn for years. There is a look about him so forlorn that it pierces me to the very core of my being. And — this is what I recall most especially — pierces me with a sense of shame, of guilty complicity. As though I were complicit in a form of murder. Regicide. As though I were standing regarding his naked body brought down — body of Agamemnon slain in his bath. I can see him still sitting there, both awesome and forlorn. And fear, love, anger, grief, a confused shame collide in me. Feelings hard even now to untangle. They were harder still to untangle those many years ago. Yes, I was glad to be moving through the ruins under cover of dark.

As the boys and I came at last full circle and were standing again at the Gate of Lions, I heard in the darkness the peeping of some small bird. It was an unlikely sound after nightfall. I had learned the Greek word for bird and I spoke it in surprise. The older boy nodded, and then ran toward the wall that flanked the gate, and I saw him clambering up it, finding foothold somehow in the cracks between the great stones. And then he came clambering down again, more slowly now and awkwardly. And he was holding out his cupped hands toward me in the half-light. I held out my own, and he put into them a tiny featherless bird — all skin and beak and still peeping timidly. I peered at it in awe, then quickly put it back into his hands. And he climbed the wall again and—carefully—returned it to its nest.

The night had grown cold. The older boy pointed at the younger now, who was shivering. I offered my scarf but he refused, in pride. And the older one gestured that we must head home. So we started back—walking fast as we could over the rough ground. When we reached the slope where the shepherd's dog had come rushing down at us, he came rushing again, again snarling—the shepherd after him. And we ran and ran and ran downhill, holding hands, but the boys stooping now and then to pick up stones to throw. We'd slow down, but then seem to hear the sound of snarling again and would run again. When we were at a safe distance, the older boy suddenly took the younger on his back, to carry him pickaback. The little one was laughing now, with a tremulous laughter that I mistook at first for weeping. He was heavy for his friend and I suggested—with gestures—that we link hands and carry him that way. So we did for a little while. But then the boy slipped off our hands and ran along on his own.

We were still quite a distance from the hotel when the two stopped and held out their hands. They were asking to be paid now, for we had come to a sidepath that was a shortcut home for them. It took me several moments to understand, for I'd assumed that they lived a little beyond the hotel—where I'd first met them. Their voices became anxious, I understood at last what they were asking, and—feeling badly not to have guessed more quickly—and wishing again that there were a better way to thank them—I paid them, and waved goodbye to them; then stumbled the rest of the way home alone.

The man who ran the hotel was astonished that I would leave in the morning without ever seeing the ruins by daylight. He had a proprietary feeling about the site, had left a scholarly book about it by my bedside. But I did take the early bus—back across the plain of Argos to Napflion (where the sea this morning was striped blue and lavender); and at Napflion I caught a bus back to Ligorio. There I learned from an old man that the festival was at

Haggus Johannus—three kilometers away. So I set out again walking. After I'd walked about a mile a truck full of soldiers came along. An old woman whom I had greeted—she was leading a goat along the road—gestured that I should hail the truck; and I did. One of the men gallantly gave me his seat in the cab.

NOTES ON CONTRIBUTORS

Paula Gunn Allen (Laguna Pueblo/Lebanese American) was born in 1939 and raised on a Spanish Land Grant in New Mexico. She has published five books of poetry. Her novel *The Woman Who Owned The Shadows* will be published by Spinsters, Ink. The editor of *Studies in American Indian Literature*, she received a post-doctoral fellowship in American Indian Studies at U.C.L.A. (1981-1982). She has also won an NEA grant for creative writing. She now teaches Native American Literature at U.C. Berkeley.

M. S. Andrews is a native Oregonian now living in San Francisco. She is working on her second novel and is completing a master's degree in Creative Writing.

Pam Annas is from a working-class background and teaches English and Women's Studies at the University of Massachusetts/Boston. The essay in *New Lesbian Writing* is part of a book in progress, *Unnaming and Renaming: A Radical Tradition of Modern American Women Poets*. She has written articles about feminist science fiction and working class fiction and has published poems in *Solana* and *Chomo-Uri*.

SDiane Bogus is a California writer formerly from Chicago. She is the author of four books, the most recent of which is *Sapphire's Sampler*, an anthology. She is currently studying for a doctorate in English at Miami University, Oxford, Ohio.

Beth Brant was born in Detroit on May 6, 1941, of a Mohawk father and a white mother. Her clan is the Turtle, her number, Strength. Her Indian name, Degonwadonti, means "many opposed to one." Out of these elements comes a complicated writer, mother, lesbian. She is most at home on her rez in Ontario. Beth edited the special issue of *Sinister Wisdom* on North American Indian women.

Karen Brodine is a typesetter and teaches creative writing. Her third book of poetry, *Illegal Assembly*, was published by Hanging

Loose Press, and she has finished another titled *Woman Sitting at the Machine Thinking*. She's a member of Radical Women and the Merle Woo Defense Committee.

LindaJean Brown. blacklesbianwoman writer. 32 yrs. living/ working in nyc. author of *The Rainbow River* (short fiction) 1980, and *jazz dancin wif mama* (narrative fiction) 1981, both from Iridian Press, NYC.

Janine Canan is a psychiatrist and poet living in Berkeley. A fourth-generation Californian, born in Los Angeles in 1942, she studied at Stanford, the University of California, and New York University School of Medicine. Her first book of poems, *Of Your Seed*, was published by Oyez Press, and her Emily Dickinson Press has published *Daughter, Who Buried the Breast of Dreams*, and *Shapes of Self*, a collection of prose poems.

Martha Courtot is a forty-one-year-old fat lesbian working-class mother of three. She is currently a coordinator for a Senior Day Care program. She has published in many women's journals and published two books of poetry, *Tribe* and *Journey*. In the works: *NightRiver* is awaiting money for printing. Tee Corinne has created a book of Martha's poems and letter fragments, as yet untitled. Her fifth book is *The Woman Moving Through the Dark*.

Janice Dabney is a native California writer who has published poetry widely but has only lately begun to work in prose. Her work has appeared in *Poetry Northwest, Occident, Seattle Review, Poet Lore*, and *Focus*. She has attended Bread Loaf Writers' Conference and will be published in a forthcoming anthology of formal verse.

doris davenport is a lesbian feminist writer who has published in several magazines and anthologies and has also self-published two books of poetry. She is working on a Ph.D. in contemporary black women's poetry.

Barbara Deming, 65, has published poems, short stories, studies of the theatre and the movies, political essays, and a prison journal. She was active in the nonviolent movement of the 60s; is now a radical feminist—and dreams of the day when the nonviolent movement and the feminist movement will become one movement.

Audrey Ewart, from Jamaica and New York, now lives in the Bay Area. She has contributed to *So's Your Old Lady, Conditions: Five*, and *The Black Lesbian Newsletter*. She has won the Grebanier Sonnet Award at Brooklyn College. "I labor for openness and growth within my writing and my life."

Elsa Gidlow, born in Yorkshire, grew up in a French Canadian village on Montreal Island. Mainly self-educated, she is a poet-philosopher who has lived for many years in northern California amid the giant redwoods. Her 1923 book *On a Gray Thread* was the first North American collection of poetry to celebrate love between women. Her recently-expanded poetry anthology *Sapphic Songs: Eighteen to Eighty* is distributed by Naiad Press. The work published here is part of her autobiography in progress.

Pamela Gray is a native New Yorker now living in Oakland. She has taught women's writing workshops in Buffalo and Boston, and is presently teaching women's studies at San Francisco State University.

Marilyn Hacker is the author of *Taking Notice, Separations*, and *Presentation Piece*, which received the National Book Award in poetry for 1975. She lives in New York City, and in 1982 became the editor of the feminist literary magazine *13th Moon*.

Esther Hawk is the pseudonym of a lesbian poet, mother, vegetable grower, teacher, attorney. She lives with her son and her lover in Vermont. Esther Hawk looks forward to a time when lesbian mothers can use their real names without threats of loss of custody.

Karla Jay majored in French and went to Paris twice, in 1978 and 1982, to do research on Vivien and Barney. Translating is a new endeavor for her and she hopes to grow up to become a Renaissance woman.

Monika Kehoe, Ph.D., Research Associate at the Center for Research and Education in Sexuality at San Francisco State University, and Associate Editor of the *Journal of Homosexuality*, is presently completing her study of lesbians over sixty-five. She also teaches a college course in autobiographical writing and is finishing her own memoirs, *The Making of a Deviant: A Model for Androgyny*, a record of her seventy-four years as a lesbian.

Yvonne Klein, an American-born lesbian, has lived and taught in Québec since 1969. She learned French in Montréal in order to translate and make available to English-speaking friends some of the considerable body of Quebeçoise lesbian-feminist writing. She expects to see her translation of Jovette Marchessault's *Lesbian Triptych* published later this year. She got a doctorate against the usual social and political odds.

Pat Kuras was born two minutes after midnight on September 30, 1954. She is a poet and writer living in Philadelphia. Her first book of poetry, *The Pinball Player*, is available from Good Gay Poets in Boston.

Jacqueline Lapidus was born in 1941 in New York City and lived in Greece for three years before settling in Paris in 1967. She now works as a magazine editor, saves up for periodic trips to Brazil, and is in the throes of a mid-life crisis. Her latest book of poems, still unpublished, is "Ultimate Conspiracy."

Mary Meigs is an American-born painter now living in Quebec, who, thanks to the courage and honesty of other lesbians, particularly Barbara Deming, was able to write her autobiography at the age of 63. She has finished a second book, *The Medusa Head*, a part of which appears in this anthology. She now considers herself a writer-painter and will continue to do both writing and painting.

Suniti Namjoshi was born in Bombay, India, in 1941. At present she is an associate professor of English at the University of Toronto. Her books of poems and fables include *The Jackass and* *the Lady, Feminist Fables*, and *The Authentic Lie*. She has also published book reviews and scholarly articles.

Caroline Overman, 37, grew up in Victoria, British Columbia. A Ph.D. in Classics, she has been a waitress, a university lecturer, and an editor of *The Blatant Image* and *WomanSpirit*.

Ida VSW Red, when not obsessing about multiple relationships, writes, performs with Mothertongue Readers' Theater, earns a living as a librarian and editor, and schemes how to become a graduate school bum again in her second fifty years.

Henry Handel Richardson is a pseudonym of the Australian writer Ethel Florence Lindsay Richardson, who lived from 1870 to 1946. A music student who later turned to writing, she spent most of her life in England. After the death of her husband, she lived for many years with Olga Roncoroni. Her works include a novel, *The Getting of Wisdom*; a trilogy based on her father's life, *The Fortunes of Richard Mahony*; and a collection of short stories, *The Adventures of Cuffy Mahony*. Dorothy Green's study of Richardson, *Ulysses Bound*, was published by the Australian National University Press at Canberra in 1973.

Renée Vivien (1877-1909) is the pseudonym of Pauline Tarn, Anglo-American poet whose account of a famous love affair with Natalie Barney, *A Woman Appeared to Me*, was re-published by Naiad Press in 1976. A collection of her stories, *The Woman of the Wolf*, translated by Karla Jay and Yvonne Klein, was recently published by the Gay Presses of New York.

Jane Rule lives on Galiano Island, off the coast of British Columbia. A Canadian citizen, she is active in the women's and gay communities, and writes articles and book reviews. Writing fiction is her main occupation. Her novels include *This Is Not For You*, *Desert of the Heart*, and *Contract with the World*. Her biographical and critical study *Lesbian Images* was an early and important contribution to lesbian literature. A collection of her essays and stories, *Outlander*, was published by Naiad Press in 1981.

Canyon Sam, lesbian, feminist, poet, writer, and performer, is a third generation San Franciscan. Active in Bay Area political and cultural work since 1975, she was a founding member of Unbound Feet, a performing collective of Chinese American women writers. An electrical contractor, she has her own business, Current Affairs Electric. Her first collection of work, *Components of Resistance*, is forthcoming.

Judy Schavrien is a psychotherapist who formerly taught humanities at the University of Chicago, where she served on the editorial staff of *The Chicago Review*. She studied with Saul Bellow and wrote a prize-winning dissertation on sexual psychology and metaphysics in *Finnegans Wake*. As a translator, she won an International Poetry Review prize for her renditions from the Dutch poet M. Vasalis. Her book of poems translated from Harry Brander's *What Rhymes with Cancer?* has been published by New Rivers Press.

Sheilah Shook is a thirty-nine-year-old Southern lesbian, feminist and therapist. Trees, friends, and loving Kay keeps her centered.

Susan Yarbrough, a native Texan and former women's studies teacher, now practices law in New York City.

RECENT LESBIAN LITERATURE, 1980-1983: A SELECTED BIBLIOGRAPHY

I. LITERATURE

Aldridge, Sarah. *The Nesting Place*. Tallahassee: Naiad Press, 1982. Fiction.

Allegra, Donna. "Butch on the Streets." *Fight Back! Feminist Resistance to Male Violence*, edited by Felice Newman and Frédérique Delacoste. Minneapolis: Cleis Press, 1981. Fiction.

———. "A Toast of Babatine." *Womanblood: Portraits of Women in Poetry and Prose*, edited by Alice O'Brien, Chrys Rasmussen and Catherine Costello. San Francisco: Continuing Saga Press, 1981. Fiction.

Allen, Paula Gunn. *Shadow Country*. Los Angeles: American Indian Studies Center, UCLA, 1982. Poems.

———. *The Woman Who Owned the Shadows*. San Francisco: Spinsters, Ink, 1983. Novel.

Allison, Dorothy. *The Women Who Hate Me*. Brooklyn: Long Haul Press, 1983. Poems.

Arobateau, Red. "Confessions of a Not-So-Ex-Alcoholic." *Lesbian Contradiction*, Summer 1983, pp. 18-20. See also Shockley interview.

Bannon, Ann. Reprints of 1950s novels: *I am a Woman, Women in the Shadows, Journey to a Woman*, and *Beebo Brinker*. Tallahassee: Naiad Press, 1982.

Barnes, Djuna. *Creatures in an Alphabet*. New York: Dial Press, 1982. Poems. Review NYTBR, 9 January 1983, p. 9.

———. *Smoke and Other Stories*. Edited by Douglas Messerli. College Park, MD.: Sun and Moon Press, 1982.

Beck, Evelyn (ed.). *Nice Jewish Girls: a Lesbian Anthology*. Watertown: Persephone Press, 1982. Reissued by The Crossing Press, 1983.

Becker, Robin. *Backtalk*. Cambridge, MA: Alice James Books, 1982. Poems.

Birtha, Becky. *For Nights Like This One: Stories of Loving Women*. East Palo Alto: Frog in the Well, 1983.

_____ . "Johnnieruth." *Extended Outlooks: The Iowa Review Collection of Contemporary Writing by Women*, No. 12 (Spring/Summer 1981). Story.

Bogus, SDiane. *Sapphire's Sampler*. WIM Publications, Box 367, College Corner, OH, 45056. Anthology.

Boucher, Sandy. *Heartwomen*. New York: Harper and Row, 1982. An account of Midwestern women including Willa Cather and Barbara Grier.

_____ . *The Notebooks of Leni Clare and Other Short Stories*. Trumansburg, N.Y.: The Crossing Press, 1982.

Bowles, Jane. *My Sister's Hand in Mine*. An Expanded Edition of the Collected Works of Jane Bowles. New York: The Ecco Press, 1982.

Brady, Maureen. *Folly*. Trumansburg, N.Y.: The Crossing Press, 1982. Excellent novel about women workers in a Carolina mill town.

Brant, Beth, ed. *A Gathering of Spirit*. Special Issue of *Sinister Wisdom* on North American Indian Women, Nos. 22/23, June 1983.

Brodine, Karen. *Illegal Assembly*. Brooklyn: Hanging Loose Press, 1980. Poems.

Broumas, Olga. *Soie Sauvage*. Port Townsend, WA.: Copper Canyon Press, 1982. Poems. Distributed by Crossing Press.

Brown, LindaJean. *jazz dancin wif mama*. New York: Iridian Press, 1981. Stories. Distributed by Turtle Grandmother Books, Box 33964, Detroit, MI 48232.

_____ . "tracin w/o papa, pensul." *Feminary* 12 (1982): 16-19. Autobiographical sketch.

Brown, Rita Mae. *Sudden Death*. New York: Bantam Books, 1983. Novel.

Bryher. *The Days of Mars. A Memoir 1940-1946*. Salem, N.H.: Marion Boyars, 1981. By H.D.'s friend Winifred Bryher. Wartime London setting.

Bulkin, Elly, ed. *Lesbian Fiction: an Anthology*. Watertown: Persephone, 1981. Excellent cross section of writers.

_____ and Joan Larkin, eds. *Lesbian Poetry: an Anthology.*
Watertown: Persephone, 1981.

Burns, Edward, ed. *Staying on Alone: Letters of Alice B.
Toklas.* New York: Liveright, 1981. PB. edition.

Cameron, Anne. *The Journey.* New York: Avon, 1982. Lesbian
Western.

Canan, Janine. *Shapes of Self.* Berkeley: Emily Dickinson
Press, 1982. Poems.

Chambers, Jane. *Burning.* New York: J. H. Press, 1983. Gothic
suspense novel.

Clarke, Cheryl. *Narratives: poems in the tradition of black
women.* New Brunswick, N.J.: Sister Books, 1982.
Distributed by Kitchen Table Press.

Clausen, Jan. *Duration.* Brooklyn: Hanging Loose Press, 1983.
Poems.

_____ . *Mother, Sister, Daughter, Lover.* Trumansburg, N.Y.:
The Crossing Press, 1980. Stories.

Cockrell, Cathy. *Undershirts and Other Stories.* Brooklyn:
Hanging Loose Press, 1982. Each story woven around an
article of clothing.

Coote, Stephen, ed. *The Penguin Book of Homosexual Verse.*
New York: Penguin, 1983. Includes Judy Grahn, Olga
Broumas, Vita Sackville-West, and Rita Mae Brown.

Corinne, Tee. *Yantras of Woman Love.* Tallahassee: Naiad
Press, 1982. Text by Jacqueline Lapidus.

Cornwell, Anita. *Black Lesbian in White America.* Tallahassee:
Naiad Press, 1983. Fiction, autobiography, essays,
interviews.

Cruikshank, Margaret, ed. *The Lesbian Path.* 2nd edition.
San Francisco: Double Axe Books, 1981. Distributed by
Naiad Press. Autobiographical sketches.

Curb, Rosemary. "Leaving the Convent." *Womanspirit,* No. 33,
August 1982, pp. 48-49.

davenport, doris. *eat thunder & drink rain.* Los Angeles: self-
published, 1982. Poems.

_____ . *it's like this.* Los Angeles: self-published, 1980. Poems.

_____ . 'Never mind the Misery/Where's the Magic?" *Sunbury* 10 (1981): 155-159. Essay.

Deming, Barbara. *Remembering Who We Are*. Pagoda Publications, 1981. Distributed by Naiad Press. Essays.

De Veaux, Alexis. "Adventures of the Dread Sisters: Miss Pinto and the Bridge." *IKON*, 2nd ser., No. 2 (Fall 1983): 36-38. Fiction.

Dillon, Millicent. *A Little Original Sin. The Life and Work of Jane Bowles*. New York: Holt, Rinehart, Winston. PB ed. 1982.

Fisher, Barbara. *Breathing Room*. Rochester: Brighton St. Press, 1982. Novel.

Forest, Katherine. *Curious Wine*. Tallahassee: Naiad Press, 1983. Novel.

Futcher, Jane. *Crush*. Boston: Little, Brown, 1981. Novel with boarding-school setting.

Garden, Nancy. *Annie on My Mind*. New York: Farrar, Straus, Giroux, 1982. Excellent young adult novel.

Gidlow, Elsa. Memoirs." *Feminist Studies* 6 (Spring 1980): 103-127. Part of autobiography in progress, *Life From Oblique Angles*.

_____ . *Sapphic Songs: Eighteen to Eighty*. Mill Valley, CA: Druid Heights Press, 1982. Distributed by Naiad.

_____ . "The Spiritual Significance of the Self-Identified Woman." *Maenad* 1 (Spring 1981): 73-79.

Glendinning, Victoria. *Vita: A Life of Vita Sackville-West*. New York: Alfred A. Knopf, 1983.

Glubka, Shirley. "Bless Me, Sister . . ." *Conditions: Nine* (1983): 46-55. Convent lesbian story.

Gómez, Alma, Cherríe Moraga and Mariana Romo-Carmona, eds. *Cuentos: Stories by Latinas*. Brooklyn: Kitchen Table Press, 1983.

Grahn, Judy, ed. *True to Life Adventure Stories*. Vol. 1. Trumansburg, N.Y.: Crossing Press, 1983. Reissue of 1978 Diana Press edition. Vol. II, Crossing Press, 1981.

_____ . *Queen of the Wands*. Trumansburg, N.Y.: Crossing Press, 1982. Poetry.

Hanscombe, Gillian. *Between Friends.* Boston: Alyson Publishing, 1982. Novel.

H.D. *The Gift.* New York: New Directions, 1982. Memoir.

———. *Hermione.* New York: New Directions, 1981. Autobiographical novel.

Johnston, Jill. *Mother Bound.* New York: Alfred A. Knopf, 1983. Autobiography.

Klepfisz, Irena. *Keeper of Accounts.* Watertown: Persephone Press, 1982. Poetry.

Koertge, Noretta. *Who Was That Masked Woman?* New York: St. Martin's, 1981. Comic adventure story.

Kreiger, Susan. *The Mirror Dance.* Identity in a Women's Community. Philadelphia: Temple University Press, 1983. The story of a Midwestern lesbian community told entirely through the women's own voices.

Livia, Anna. *Relatively Norma.* London: Onlywomen Press, n.d. Novel.

Lorde, Audre. *Zami: A New Spelling of My Name.* Watertown: Persephone Press, 1982. Autobiography.

Lynch, Lee. *Toothpick House.* Tallahassee: Naiad Press, 1983. Fiction.

McDaniel, Judith. "Coming Out: Ten Years of Change." *Ariadne's Thread. A Collection of Contemporary Women's Journals,* edited by Lyn Lifshin. New York: Harper and Row, 1982.

———. *November Woman.* Brooklyn: Long Haul Press, 1983. Poetry.

Manahan, Nancy. "A Lesbian Ex-Nun Meets Her Sisters." *Common Lives/Lesbian Lives,* Summer, 1983, pp. 88-91.

Martin, Del and Phyllis Lyon. *Lesbian/Woman.* New edition with ten year update. 1972-1982. New York: Bantam, 1983.

Manning, Rosemary. *A Time and a Time.* London: Calder and Boyars, 1982. Orig. pub. 1971 under pseud. Sarah Davys. Autobiography.

Meigs, Mary. *Lily Briscoe: A Self-Portrait.* Vancouver: Talonbooks, 1981. Autobiography. Meigs is featured in Issue 5 of

The Radical Reviewer, Winter 81-82; cover photo; interview with Barbara Herringer; book reviewed by Cy-Thea Sand.

_____ . Excerpt from *The Medusa Head*. *The Body Politic*, October-November, 1983. Autobiography.

Miner, Valerie. *Blood Sisters*. New York: St. Martin's Press, 1982.

_____ . *Movement*. Trumansburg, N.Y.: Crossing Press, 1982. Novel.

Moraga, Cherríe. *Loving in the War Years*. Boston: South End Press, 1983. Poems, stories, essays.

_____ and Gloria Anzaldúa, eds. *This Bridge Called My Back: Writings by Radical Women of Color*. Watertown: Persephone Press, 1981.

Nestle, Joan. "Lesbian Memories 1: Riis Park, New York City, ca 1960." *Common Lives/Lesbian Lives*, Summer 1983, pp. 14-16.

Noda, Barbara. "Sayonara Amor." *Common Lives/Lesbian Lives*, Summer 1983, pp. 74-79. Story.

Pratt, Minnie Bruce. *The Sound of One Fork*. Durham: Night Heron Press, 1982. Poetry.

Rich, Adrienne. *A Wild Patience Has Taken Me This Far*. New York: Norton, 1981. Poetry.

Rich, Cynthia. "The Women in the Tower." *Trivia* 2 (Spring 1983): 36-44. Black women meet with Boston Housing Authority.

Rossetti, Christina. *Goblin Market*. Boston: David R. Godine, 1981. Reissue of 1862 edition.

Rule, Jane. Reprints of novels: *This is not for You, Desert of the Heart, Contract With the World*. Tallahassee: Naiad Press, 1982.

_____ . *Outlander*. Tallahassee: Naiad Press, 1981. Essays and short stories.

Russ, Joanna. *The Adventures of Alyx*. New York: Pocketbooks, 1983. Fantasy.

_____ . *On Strike Against God*. Brooklyn: Out and About Books, 1980. Novel.

Segrest, Mab. *Living in a House I Do Not Own*. Durham: Night Heron Press, 1982. Poetry.

Shelley, Martha. *Lovers and Mothers*. Oakland: Sefir, 1981. Poetry.

Shockley, Ann Allen. *The Black and White of It*. Tallahassee: Naiad Press, 1980.

———. *Say Jesus and Come to Me*. New York: Avon, 1982. Novel.

Smith, Barbara, ed. *Home Girls: a Black Feminist Anthology*. Brooklyn: Kitchen Table Press, 1983.

Stanley, Julia Penelope and Susan J. Wolfe, eds. *The Coming Out Stories*. Watertown: Persephone Press, 1980.

Stein, Gertrude. *Blood on the Dining Room Floor*. Edited by John Gill. Berkeley: Creative Arts Books, 1982. Murder Mystery set in the French village where Stein and Toklas had their country house.

———. *The Yale Gertrude Stein*. Selections with an introduction by Richard Kostelanetz. New Haven: Yale University Press, 1980.

Steward, Samuel, *Chapters from an Autobiography*. San Francisco: Grey Fox Press, 1981. Contains wonderful sketch of Gertrude and Alice.

Swallow, Jean. "Toto, I have a Feeling We're Not in Kansas Anymore." *Lesbian Contradiction. A Journal of Irreverent Feminism*. No. 3, Summer 1983, pp. 1-4. Story.

Taylor, Valerie. *Prism*. Tallahassee: Naiad Press, 1981. Novel about older lesbians.

———. Reprints of novels from 1950s: *Journey to Fulfillment, A World Without Men* and *Return to Lesbos*. Tallahassee: Naiad Press, 1982.

Tsui, Kitty. *The Words of a Woman Who Breathes Fire*. San Francisco: Spinsters, Ink, 1983. Prose and poetry.

Vivien, Renée. *The Woman of the Wolf*. Trans. Karla Jay and Yvonne Klein. New York: Gay Presses of New York, 1983.

Walker, Alice. *The Color Purple*. New York: Harcourt, Brace, Jovanovich, 1982.

Warner, Sylvia Townsend. *Scenes of Childhood.* New York: Viking, 1982.

———. *Letters.* Edited by William Maxwell. New York: Viking, 1983. Reviewed by Mollie Panter-Downes, *New Yorker,* 30 May 1983, pp. 98-101.

Wilson, Barbara. *Ambitious Women.* Argyle, N.Y.: Spinsters, Ink, 1982.

Wolff, Charlotte. *Hindsight.* London: Quartet Books, 1982. Autobiography of a lesbian now in her eighties, a psychiatrist who fled from Nazi Germany to England.

Woman Poet. The East. Vol. 2. Reno: Women-in-Literature, 1981. Includes Adrienne Rich and Audre Lorde.

Woolf, Virginia. *Melymbrosia.* Edited by Louise De Salvo. New York: The New York Public Library, 1982. First version of *The Voyage Out;* contains more lesbian content than Woolf's first published novel.

II. CRITICISM

Allen, Dan and Margaret Cruikshank. "Team-Teaching Gay and Lesbian Literature: a Conversation." *The Radical Teacher.* Special gay studies issue, No. 24 (Fall, 1983).

Allen, Paula Gunn. "Judy Grahn: the Tribal Connection." *Contact II* (Winter-Spring 1983): 7-9.

———. *Studies in American Indian Literature.* Critical Essays and Course Designs. New York: Modern Language Association, 1983.

Annas, Pamela. " 'Drunk with Chastity': the Poetry of Renée Vivien." *Women's Studies: an Interdisciplinary Journal* (Spring 1983).

———. "A Poetry of Survival: Unnaming and Renaming in the Poetry of Audre Lorde, Pat Parker, Sylvia Plath and Adrienne Rich." *Colby College Library Quarterly* 23 (March 1982): 9-25.

Atwood, Margaret. *Second Words.* Selected Critical Prose. Toronto: Anasi Press, 1982. Essay on Millett's *Flying.*

Barracks, Barbara. "Klepfisz Bridges Past and Present."
    Womanews, May 1983, p. 11. Review of Keeper of
    Accounts.
Barrington, Judith. Interview with Audre Lorde. Advocate, No.
    368, 26 May 1983, pp. 39-40.
Birtha, Becky. Review of The Color Purple. New Women's
    Times, Feminist Review, July/August 1983, p. 4.
_____ . Review of Zami and Chosen Poems by Audre Lorde.
    New Women's Times, Feminist Review, June 1983, pp. 4-5.
Bulkin, Elly. "An Interchange on Feminist Criticism on
    'Dancing Through the Minefield' " Feminist Studies 8
    (Fall 1982): 635-54. On homophobia and racism in feminist
    literary criticism.
_____ and Barbara Smith. Feminist Perspectives on Anti-
    Semitism and Racism: Two Essays. Brooklyn: Long Haul
    Press, 1983.
Canaan, Andrea. Review of Zami. Coming up! [San Francisco],
    February 1983, p. 19.
Cantor, Aviva. Interview with Evelyn Beck, editor of Nice
    Jewish Girls: a Lesbian Anthology. Lilith 10 (Winter 1983):
    10-14.
Cheatham, Evelyn. "The Words of a Woman Who Breathes
    Fire." Morena I, April 1983, p. 6. Interview with Kitty
    Tsui.
Clarke, Cheryl, Jewelle Gomez, Evelynn Hammonds, Bonnie
    Johnson, and Linda Powell. "Black Women on Black
    Women Writers: Conversations and Questions."
    Conditions: Nine (1983): 88-137.
Clausen, Jan. A Movement of Poets: Thoughts on Poetry and
    Feminism. Brooklyn: Long Haul Press, 1982.
Cliff, Michelle. "Object into Subject: Some Thoughts on the
    Work of Black Women Artists." Heresies No. 15 (1982):
    34-40.
_____ . Review of This Bridge Called My Back: Writings by
    Radical Women of Color. Sinister Wisdom 19 (Winter
    1982): 26-31.

Cornell, Michiyo. "Invisible Among the Invisible." *Azalea* 4 (Spring/Summer 1981): 6-8.

Craven, Rhonda. "Gaining an Understanding of Womyn of Color." *SisterSource: a Midwest Lesbian/Feminist Newspaper*, 15 December 1981, p. 6. Review of *This Bridge Called My Back* and *Black Lesbians: an Annotated Bibliography*.

Cruikshank, Margaret, ed. *Lesbian Studies*. Old Westbury, N.Y.: The Feminist Press, 1982. Contains several essays on literature.

————— . "Notes on Recent Lesbian Autobiographical Writing." *Journal of Homosexuality* 8 (Fall 1982): 19-26.

Daniel, Rosemary. "The Poet Who Found Her Own Way." Review of *Zami* and *Chosen Poems, Old and New*. *New York Times Book Review*, 19 December 1982, p. 12.

Decarnin, Camilla. "Ann Bannon." *Advocate*, 28 April 1983, pp. 40-41. On the 1950s heroine Beebo Brinker.

DeSalvo, Louise. "Lighting the Cave: The Relationship between Vita Sackville-West and Virginia Woolf." *Signs* 8 (Winter 1982): 195-214. DeSalvo is editing the letters of Woolf and Sackville-West.

Diehl, Joanne. "Rich's *Common Language* and the Woman Poet." *Feminist Studies* 6 (1980): 530-46.

Doughty, Frances. "Djuna Barnes: What Are We To Make of Her? Problems in Lesbian and Feminist Research." Panel at National Women's Studies Association, June 1983, Ohio State. Other participants: Carolyn Allen, University of Washington; Mary Lynn Broe, SUNY Binghamton.

Edel, Deborah, Clare Potter, and JR Roberts. "A Guide to Current Lesbian Periodicals." *Lesbian Herstory Archives Newsletter* 6 (July 1980): 19-20.

Faderman, Lillian. "Ignoring Attachments." Review of Engen's biography of Kate Greenaway and Battiscomb's biography of Christina Rossetti, focusing on their heterocentric bias. *Gay Studies Newsletter* 9 (November 1982): 12-14.

————— . *Scotch Verdict.* Miss Pirie and Miss Woods v. Dame

Cumming. New York: Quill Books, 1983.

———. *Surpassing the Love of Men: Romantic Friendship and Love Between Women from the Renaissance to the Present*. New York: Morrow, 1981. A pioneering work; essential reading for lesbian literary and intellectual history.

Finke, Nancy. "Novel Shows That Life Begins at 65." *Sister-Source: A Midwest Lesbian/Feminist Newspaper*, 1 November 1981, p. 6. Review of *Prism* by Valerie Taylor.

Frye, Marilyn. *The Politics of Reality. Essays in Feminist Theory*. Trumansburg, N.Y.: Crossing Press, 1983.

Gambill, Sue Dove. "Olga Broumas on Continuity and Change." *Sojourner*, October 1982, p. 10. Interview.

Gomez, Jewelle. *"A Cultural Legacy Denied and Discovered: Black Lesbians in Fiction by Women." Home Girls*, edited by Barbara Smith. Brooklyn: Kitchen Table Press, 1983. Excerpt printed in *Womanews*. July/August, 1983, p. 14.

———. Review of *Zami. Conditions: Nine* (1983): 168-72.

Goodman, Jan. "Out of the Closet, But Paying the Price: Lesbian and Gay Characters in Children's Literature." *Interracial Books for Children Bulletin* 14, Nos. 3 and 4 (1982): 13-15. Some good work appearing, but stereotypes and inaccuracies persist.

Grier, Barbara, ed. *The Lesbian in Literature*. 3rd ed., Tallahassee: Naiad Press, 1981. Bibliography. Essential source.

Griffin, Susan. *Made from this Earth: an Anthology of Writings*. New York: Harper and Row, 1982.

Hammond, Karla. Interview with Audre Lorde. *American Poetry Review* 9 (1980): 18-21.

Henry, Alice. "Images of Lesbian Sexuality." Interview with Tee Corinne." *off our backs*, April 1983, pp. 10-12.

Hogan, Candace. Interview with Blanche Cook. *IKON*, Fall/Winter, 1982-83, pp. 54-59.

Homosexuality: Sacrilege, Vision, Politics. Special issue of *Salmagundi* [Skidmore], Fall/Winter, 1982-83. Laced with

homophobia, but interesting articles by Jill Johnston and
Catharine Stimpson.

Hull, Gloria T. "Researching Alice Dunbar-Nelson." *Black
Women's Studies*. Edited by Gloria T. Hull, Barbara
Smith, and Patricia Bell Scott. Old Westbury, N.Y.: The
Feminist Press, 1982.

Jay, Karla. "Decoding Djuna Barnes and *The Ladies Almanack*."
Gay News [Philadelphia], 14 July 1983, pp. 7-8.

_____ . "A Lesbian/Feminist Tour of Paris." Three hundred
slides and music on pacifists and others in the twenties.

JEB [Joan E. Biren]. "Lesbian Photography—Seeing Through
Our Own Eyes." *Studies in Visual Communication* 9
(Spring 1983): 81-95.

Jumpcut. Special issue on lesbians and film. Nos. 24 and 25
(1981).

Kaye, Melanie. "Culture-Making: Lesbian Classics in the Year
2000?" *Sinister Wisdom* 13 (Spring 1980).

Keohane, Nannerl O., Michelle Z. Rosaldo and Barbara Gelpi,
eds. *Feminist Theory. A Critique of Ideology*. Chicago:
University of Chicago Press, 1982. Reactions to Adrienne
Rich article "On Compulsory Heterosexuality and Lesbian
Existence" by Ann Ferguson, Jacqueline Zita, and Kathryn
Pyne Addelson.

Klein, Yvonne. "What Makes Jane Rule Run?" Interview. *Gay
News*, 23 December 1982, p. 14.

Krouskoff, Margaret. "Combining Theory and Practice:
Contributions to the Development of Lesbian Studies
within Academic Institutions." Senior thesis, Women's
Studies, University of California, Berkeley, 1983.
Includes annotated bibliography.

Lesbian Writing and Publishing. Special issue of *Sinister
Wisdom*. No. 13 (Spring 1980).

McAllister, Pam, ed. *Reweaving the Web of Life: Feminism
and Nonviolence*. Philadelphia: New Society Publishers,
1982. Includes Mab Segrest interview with Barbara
Deming and Karla Jay essay on Natalie Barney.

Macdonald, Barbara. "The Development of the Contemporary Lesbian Short Story." *New Women's Times, Feminist Review,* June 1981, pp. 8-9.

———. "Examining Attitudes Towards Aging." *New Women's Times,* May 1983, p. 8.

———. "The Power of the Old Woman." *New Women's Times, Feminist Review,* May 1983, p. 1. Discusses *Sister Gin, Prism,* and *As We Are Now.*

McDaniel, Judith. Interview with Valerie Miner. *New Women's Times, Feminist Review,* January-February 1983, pp. 8-9.

McNaron, Toni. "Echoes of Virginia Woolf." *Women's Studies International Forum,* Fall 1983.

Manahan, Nancy. "Future Old Maids and Pacifist Agitators: The Story of Tracy Mygatt and Frances Witherspoon." *Women's Studies Quarterly* 10 (Spring 1982): 10-13. Two early members of the War Resisters League who were together for more than sixty years.

Marcus, Jane. "Liberty, Sorority, Misogny" in *The Representation of Women in Fiction,* edited by Carolyn Heilbrun. Baltimore: Johns Hopkins University Press, 1983.

——— ed. *Virginia Woolf: A Feminist Slant.* Lincoln: University of Nebraska Press, 1983. See essay by Emily Jensen on *Mrs. Dalloway* and essay by Louise DeSalvo on Vita Sackville-West and Woolf.

———. Review of Grace Radin's *Virginia Woolf: The Years. Virginia Woolf Miscellany,* No. 20 (Spring 1983): 4-5. Notes some lesbian passages in ms. version of *The Years.*

Meigs, Mary. *The Medusa Head.* Vancouver: Talonbooks, 1983. Autobiography.

———. "Speaking Hard Truths with Their Whole Selves." *The Body Politic,* April 1983, pp. 33-34. On writing by lesbians of color.

Morgan, Yarrow. Review of *Zami. Hurricane Alice* I (Spring 1983), p. 11.

Mullen, Pat. Review of *Queen of the Wands. Women Library*

Workers Journal, March 1983, p. 18.

Mushrcom, Merrill. Review of Ann Shockley's *The Black and White of It*. *Feminary* 12, No. 1, pp. 152-161.

Namjoshi, Suniti. "Snow White and Rose Green: or Some Notes on Sexism, Racism, and the Craft of Writing." *Canadian Women's Studies* 4 (Winter 1982): 11-15.

Nestle, Joan. "Desire So Big It Had To Be Brave: Ann Bannon's Novels." *Womanews* [New York City], March 1983, 12-13.

Oktenberg, Adrian. "The Mysticism of Judy Grahn." *The Women's Review of Books*, Summer 1983, pp. 6-8.

Orta, Lisa. *A New Woman Hero: A Study of the Heroic Journey in Five Twentieth Century Lesbian Novels*. MA thesis, San Francisco State University, 1981.

Parkerson, Michelle. Review of *Narratives: Poems in the Tradition of Black Women*. *off our backs*, May 1983, p. 25.

Patton, Cindy. "The Politics of Lesbian Writing: a Conversation with Elly Bulkin." *Gay Community News*, 23 January 1982, pp. 8-9.

Platt, Charles. "Profile: Joanna Russ." *Asimov Science Fiction Magazine* 7 (March 1983): 30-45.

Porter, Veneita. "Cheryl Clarke: Poetry, Politics, and Black Lesbian Aesthetic." *Gay Community News*, 5 March 1983, pp. 8-9.

"Racism is the Issue." *Heresies*, No. 15 (1982). Authors include Donna Allegra, Michelle Cliff, Audre Lorde, and Pat Parker.

Radical Teacher. Special gay/lesbian studies issue. Fall 1983.

Resources for Feminist Research 12 (March 1983). The lesbian issue. Canadian focus.

Rich, Cynthia. "Aging, Agism, and Feminist Avoidance." *New Women's Times, Feminist Review*, May 1983, p. 10.

Roberts, JR. *Black Lesbians: an Annotated Bibliography*. Tallahassee: Naiad Press, 1981.

Rosenfeld, Marthe. "Language and Vision of a Lesbian Feminist Utopia in Wittig's *Les Guérillières*.

Frontiers 6 (Spring/Summer 1981): 6-9.

Rule, Jane. *Lesbian Images.* Trumansburg, N.Y.: Crossing
Press, 1982. Biography and criticism. Excellent introduction. First published 1975.

Rupp, Leila. Review of *Surpassing the Love of Men. Women's
Studies Review* 5 (Spring 1983): 12-13.

Russ, Joanna. *How to Suppress Women's Writing.* Austin:
University of Texas Press, 1983.

Schuster, Marilyn. "Strategies for Survival: The Subtle Subver-
sion of Jane Rule." *Feminist Studies* 7 (Fall 1981): 431-50.

Seajay, Carol. Review of *Folly* by Maureen Brady. *Plexus,*
April 1983.

Secor, Cynthia. "Gertrude Stein: the Complex Force of her
Femininity." *Women, the Arts, and the 1920's in Paris and
New York,* edited by Kenneth Wheeler and Virginia Lee
Lussier. New Brunswick, N.J.: Transaction Books, 1982.

————— . "The Question of Gertrude Stein." *American Novelists
Revisited. Essays in Feminist Criticism,* edited by Fritz
Fleischmann. Boston: G. K. Hall, 1982.

Shaktini, Namascar. "Displacing the Phallic Subject: Wittig's
Lesbian Writing." *Signs* 8 (Autumn 1982): 29-44.

Shockley, Ann Allen. "A Different Kind of Black Lesbian
Writer." Interview with Red Jordan Arobateau. *Sinister
Wisdom* 21 (Fall 1982): 35-39. Issue also contains work by
Arobateau.

Shore, Rima. "Remembering Sophia Parnok, 1885-1933."
Conditions: Six (Summer 1980): 177-93. Russian lesbian
poet.

Skurnik, Jennifer. "At Last, Lesbian Characters for the Stage."
off our backs, April 1983, p. 13. On Jane Chambers.

Simmons, Judy. "The Many Faces of Audre Lorde." *Contact II,*
Winter-Spring 1983, pp. 44-46. Interview. Issue also
includes reviews of *The Cancer Journals* and *Chosen
Poems, Old and New.*

Smith, Jane S. *Elsie deWolfe: A Life in the High Style.* New
York: Atheneum, 1982. American lesbians in Paris.

Sorrel,, Lorraine. Interview with Cherríe Moraga and Barbara
    Smith about *This Bridge Called My Back*. *off our backs*,
    April 1982, 4-5. *This Bridge* reviewed in same issue by
    Deborah Aslan Jamieson.
———— and Susan Sojourner. Interview with Maureen Brady.
    off our backs, April 1983, pp. 14-16.
Stigers, Eva. "Sappho's Private World." *Women's Studies* 8
    (1981): 47-63. Sappho's poetry "fundamentally different
    from that of the male lyric poets."
Stimpson, Catharine. "Zero Degree Deviancy: the Lesbian
    Novel in English." *Critical Inquiry* 8 Writing and Sexual
    Difference (Winter 1981): 363-79. Lively, stimulating
    essay; subtitle misleading: only a few novels are treated,
    including *The Well of Loneliness* and *Lover*.
Tilchen, Maida. Interview with Ann Bannon. *Gay Community
    News*, 8 January 1983. See also Andrea Lowenstein's
    article "Sad Stories: a Reflection on the Fiction of Ann
    Bannon." *GCN*, 24 May 1980, p. 8.
Vicinus, Martha. " 'One Life to Stand Beside Me': Emotional
    Conflicts in First-Generation College Women in England."
    Feminist Studies 8 (Fall 1982): 603-628.
Watkins, Tanya. Review of Doris Davenport's *it's like this*.
    Motheroot Journal, Winter 1982, p. 6.
Zimmerman, Bonnie. "Daughters of Darkness: the Lesbian
    Vampire in Film." *Jumpcut* 24-25 (March 1981): 23-24.
    Special issue on lesbians and film.
———— . "Exiting from Patriarchy: the Lesbian Novel of
    Development." *The Voyage In: Fictions of Female Develop-
    ment*, edited by Elizabeth Abel, et al. Hanover, N.H.:
    University Press of New England, 1983.
———— . "Is 'Chloe Liked Olivia' a Lesbian Plot?" *Women's
    Studies International Forum* 6 (1983): 169-75.
———— . "What Has Never Been: an Overview of Lesbian
    Feminist Literary Criticism." *Feminist Studies* 7 (Fall
    1981): 451-76.

III. PERIODICALS

Common Lives/Lesbian Lives. A lesbian-feminist quarterly. Box 1553, Iowa City, IA 52244.

Conditions. A feminist magazine of writings by women with an emphasis on writing by lesbians. Box 56, Van Brunt Station, Brooklyn, NY 11215.

Feminary. A Feminist Journal for the South Emphasizing Lesbian Visions. Box 954, Chapel Hill, NC 27514.

Focus. Lesbian literary journal. c/o Paula Bennett, Beaver Pond Rd., Lincoln, MA 01773.

Gay Studies Newsletter. Published by the Gay Caucus of the Modern Language Association. Contains news and Reviews of lesbian literature. Ed. Michael Lynch, Department of English, 7 Kings College Circle, University of Toronto, Ontario M5S 1A1.

Onyx. Black Lesbian Newsletter. 1442A Walnut St., #307, Berkeley, CA 94709.

Sinister Wisdom. A Journal of Words and Pictures for the Lesbian Imagination in All Women. Box 1023, Rockland, ME 04841.

Grey Fox Books

John Coriolan	*Christy Dancing*
Margaret Cruikshank	*New Lesbian Writing*
Daniel Curzon	*Human Warmth & Other Stories*
Guy Davenport	*Herakleitos and Diogenes* *The Mimes of Herondas*
Edward Dorn	*Selected Poems*
Lawrence Ferlinghetti	*The Populist Manifesto*

Allen Ginsberg	*Composed on the Tongue*
	The Gates of Wrath: Rhymed Poems
	  1948–1952
	Gay Sunshine Interview
	  (with Allen Young)

Howard Griffin	*Conversations with Auden*
Richard Hall	*Couplings: A Book of Stories* *Three Plays for a Gay Theater*
Jack Kerouac	*Heaven & Other Poems*
Stanley Lombardo	*Parmenides and Empedocles*
Michael McClure	*Hymns to St. Geryon & Dark Brown*
Frank O'Hara	*Early Writing* *Poems Retrieved* *Standing Still and Walking* *in New York*
Charles Olson	*The Post Office*

Eric Rofes	*"I Thought People Like That*
	  Killed Themselves"—*Lesbians,*
	  Gay Men & Suicide

Michael Rumaker	*A Day and a Night at the Baths* *My First Satyrnalia*
Gary Snyder	*He Who Hunted Birds in His Father's* *Village: Dimensions of a Haida Myth*